Castles of Colorado

CASTLES OF COLORADO

Scandals, Hauntings, and Tales of the Past

Ann Westerberg

Ann Westerberg
June, 2009

JOHNSON BOOKS
BOULDER

To Decker Westerberg
for his constant support

Published by Johnson Books, a Big Earth Publishing company.
3005 Center Green Drive, Suite 220 · Boulder, Colorado 80301.
1-800-258-5830
E-mail: books@bigearthpublishing.com
www.bigearthpublishing.com

Cover and text design by Rebecca Finkel

9   8   7   6   5   4   3   2   1

Library of Congress Cataloging-in-Publication Data

Westerberg, Ann.
Castles of Colorado : scandals, hauntings,
and tales of the past / Ann Westerberg.
p. cm.
Includes bibliographical references and index.
ISBN 978-1-55566-417-6
1. Castles—Colorado—Anecdotes. 2. Haunted castles—Colorado—Anecdotes.
3. Historic buildings—Colorado—Anecdotes. 4. Scandals—Colorado—Anecdotes.
5. Ghosts—Colorado—Anecdotes. 6. Colorado—History, Local—Anecdotes.
7. Colorado—History—Anecdotes. 8. Colorado—Biography—Anecdotes. I. Title.
F777.W47 2008
978.8'03—dc22
2008003119

Printed in China through World Print, Ltd.

Contents

Preface

Perhaps the most romantic idea in the world is a castle, along with all its baggage. There is hardly a children's fairy tale lacking this high-on-the-hill destination wherein the occupants are living happily ever after. Thus, from our very beginnings, we are saturated with the propaganda of castles; propaganda thoroughly imbedded into our collective psyches—certainly mine.

It's no surprise that along with the history of the structures themselves comes the history of the era, as well as of the areas in which they were built. Building a castle and purchasing the surrounding land were heavy expenses necessarily involving persons of means, imagination, and enterprise. These entrepreneurs were the pioneers and developers of Colorado, and their names are often found on our buildings and streets. A biographical sketch of that person or persons seems an integral piece of the castle lore, adding a fourth dimension of personality to each castle. Many of these structures now stand as monuments to the creation of our state.

It seems that a maturing Colorado had timed it perfectly. Gold, silver, and coal were the varicose veins of her hills, bulging with riches for those brave and foolish enough to devote themselves to the quest. Miners coming West were lured by the siren songs of wealth, as were the neophyte railroads, nuzzling into the area like pigs to a trough. Miners, striking it rich, were filling the pockets of the tradesmen and capitalists, and especially those who had invested in real estate. Henry Brown, homesteading 160 acres, created Brown's Bluff, now Capitol Hill, which was soon studded with massive homes in which former penniless farm boys and descendants of royalty now lived side by side. Grant Street itself was known world-wide as Gold Street, America's wealthiest block.

According to Edith Kohl in her book *Denver's Historic Mansions*, "Denver became known from San Francisco to Paris as the City of Mansions." But beyond the mansion, we had the castle, and the castle *builder*—the ultimate dreamer. Dreamers, then and today, are those of us who have never quite left our childhood behind.

Unlike the original goal of a castle as fortification, the Colorado castles were erected as the solidification of a dream as well as a declaration of power—the home of a monarch. It was the crow of the cock. And many a cock ran the henhouse by his own set of rules, often making for maverick—but never-the-less interesting—personages.

Appealing to my own streak of curiosity, I've included some of the scandalous activity found in my research. Not all chapters contain scandal, but power can beget some strange bedfellows. Additionally, some castles have former occupants who just haven't left. This too has been noted, for those interested in the paranormal.

Also included are castles no longer standing but still of historic interest none the less. Structures, even of stone, can eventually decay or lose their form and return to being a part of the natural landscape. However, the creativity and innovation involved in the origin of these grand buildings inevitably planted other still viable seeds. After all is said and done, the only things indestructible on earth are ideas.

Not all castles are accessible, as some are private homes. Nevertheless, there are many you can visit if you wish to do so. This book contains directions, accessible days, phone numbers, and often websites. Many wonderful moments in life are sometimes offered, from simply having tea to wedding your beloved.

Thus we have here a guide book/history book trimmed in romance, scandal, and heroism. The castles have often outlasted their makers, but they stand as a testament to foresight, bravery, often recklessness, and foremost, enterprise. My aim for this book is to make it deliciously didactic. Bon appétit.

Acknowledgments

The cooperation and enthusiasm I encountered on this project truly amazed me. I was very touched by these people's devotion to the history of either the person who created the castle, or the castle itself. Their overall generosity made my project a delightful adventure.

The Cherokee Castle's two devoted docents, Meg Anderson and John Lake, have not only been on the staff for some twenty-three years, but were good and trusted friends of Tweet Kimball, the Grand Dame of the castle. Their insight and friendship have been invaluable. Terry Williams, executive director of Cherokee, welcomed my presence, and allowed me to photograph there at a time the castle was closed to the public.

Dunafon Castle has been restored to its original glory by Mike Dunafon, a very hands-on owner, and his wife, Debbie Matthews. He not only supplied me with endless information, but with a full disc of glorious pictures taken by himself, with permission to use them. (See cover photo.) Thank you, Annette Gilman, for the info and tour there.

For the Castle Marne, owners Diane and Jim Peiker have spent hours giving me the history. The Peikers also referred me to Dr. Charles O. Brantigan who has spent years tracking the history of the architect, William Lang. Doctor Brantigan also very generously shared his updated biographical information, which was not only years, but miles, in the making.

I can't say enough good things about Jerry Priddy, who with his wife, Esther, has owned and lived in the Richthofen Castle for some twenty-three years. Often, he took time out to talk with me, give me leads for information, and read and instruct me on his castle, when I know the Priddys are constantly pestered about their digs. And thanks to Sally Cooper Murray for her insight into the Pereyni family.

And to Chris Vitt, I am grateful for her tours, history, and personal experiences, in and of the South Broadway Christian Church, and to Pastor Mark Pumphrey as well. Who would have thought that so much history and mystery lurked in that wonderful old building.

Jamie Noebel of the Highlands Ranch Community Association, with mind-boggling efficiency, took care of procuring the photos (hers, actually), and for reading my chapter on the Springer Castle, now known as the Highlands Ranch Mansion. I also thank Caroline Smith, president of the H.R. Historical Society for the ghost stories and related experiences. And a big hug and many thanks to Sonya Ellingboe, friend and columnist for *The Littleton Independent*, for turning me on to Springer Castle.

Obtaining photos and permission for a chapter on Glen Eyrie was a fearsome challenge until I met Toby Reed, executive director there. Toby got the permission from The Navigators for the chapter, and supplied me with a disc of photos, which I *really* appreciated.

Many thanks to Peggy Yager of the Manitou Springs Historical Society, and Margaret Johnson, docent of Miramont Castle, for their cooperation. Theirs is such a fascinating castle, and so *haunted*. Yum.

Bishop's Castle is truly known all over Colorado, with its fame actually spreading throughout the world. I thank Jim Bishop for taking the time out to stop and give me his time and history.

Dear Cano is a gentle, sharing man who has produced an actual piece of folk art solely by himself. I hope his castle brings him more than just renown.

Meme and Doc Hardin were more than generous in sharing their stunning project with me—Hardin Castle, a private home that just happens to be a castle.

The Lion and the Rose Castle is a glorious masterpiece and I thank the owner and agent for their input on a fascinating piece of property. Jeff Ordoney took time out to read and correct my writing, and to send me high resolution pictures of this incredible building. Many thanks, Jeff.

Susan McEvoy, with the gargantuan job of organizing tours for the restored Redstone Castle, took time out to read my chapter and the re-write, and to return them post haste. Having worked for the castle for eight years, she was vital to my getting it right. And a more interesting, knowledgeable docent you'll never find. Thanks, Susan.

Much gratitude goes to B. J. Ellison of Jefferson County Open Space. I "happened" to get him on the phone when calling for directions to their office. And he "happened" to be the expert on the history of John Brisben Walker, the man I was researching. (Chills.) I thank B. J. for literally hours of perusing Walker information that he had gathered himself, and for then reading my chapters for accuracy. J. Brisben Walker was responsible for three castles and three chapters: River Front, Falcon, and the Summer White House.

Visiting the sites of Hovenweep, I met Chris Nickel, park ranger. After I staggered back from a two-mile walk in 96 degree heat, he took pity and e-mailed me the pictures of Cutthroat Castle, the one in Colorado. *I* got the pics of the Utah Hovenweep Castle, but hey, what did the Anazasi know about borders?

I gathered much of my information on the Crystal Castle, or Ice Palace in Leadville from the book by Darlene Godat. Darlene herself looked over my chapter and helped me with the sequence and accuracy. Many thanks to Ray Stamps, president of the Leadville Historic Society, for getting me permission to photograph the replications.

The information on Kittredge Castle was gleaned from newspaper reports. I owe many thanks to the personnel in the Western History Department of the Denver Public Library, and particularly to Coi Drummond-Gehrig for her help with historical pictures. And to Steve Grinstead of the Colorado Historical Society, I'm very grateful that you sent me to someone interested in my subject.

Julia Kanellos is the palace historian at The Brown Palace and took time out to read and correct my chapter on her hotel. Although The Brown was later designated a "non-castle" and deleted, Julia was thoroughly knowledgeable about the smallest detail, and she was willing to clear up any questions I had, with a clear answer. I learned a lot about Denver history studying Mr. Henry Brown.

The architect, J. B. B. Benedict, was a Littletonite, and thanks to Lorena Donahue, the Deputy Director and Curator of the Littleton Historical Museum, I got many details on a very interesting personage.

I'd loudly like to thank my editor and publisher, Mira Perrizo for all her work, her patience, and her cooperation. She made a daunting job easier than expected. But the thing I love best about Mira is that she let me paint the chapters with my own colors. And speaking of colors, I'm thrilled with the cover and text design, thanks to Rebecca Finkel. Design of the cover is always a heart-stopper.

Last, and perhaps most, I'd like to thank my husband Decker. His unselfish endorsement and enthusiasm for "castleing" and for the book has made this a vehicle of good times for the two of us in spite of my hogging the computer and spending hours off in my own world.

Introduction

Just what is a castle? We speak of a person's home as his castle, or we build castles in the air when we mentally conjure up our innermost desires. Castles are ideals and places of safety and comfort. They're slathered with opulence, dredged with knights in armor and courtly obeisance, and heavily veiled in romance.

In person, castles are active, energetic entities, throbbing with internal forces that are powered by portraits of ancient ancestors and silent suits of dented armor holding lances long washed of their gore. Massive bulwarks of stone conceal secret passages, peopled now with spirits either bent on vicious revenge or wailing in the wind for a lost lover.

Castles are alive and exciting and adventurous, unlike the prissy palace, home of the "proper" regency with its walls lined with hand-painted china and its cavernous rooms iced with chandeliers of imported crystal. A castle is a fortress—masculine to a fault. It's as primitive and intriguing as that dumb-dumb who can't pass freshman English, but at six-foot-five with a mop of dark, curly hair, and a physique like a buffalo, certainly *does* have his appeal.

And, ah, the moat (perhaps now eroded and leaving only a suggestion of what once was) with its message, "Only those I choose will be able to breech my interior." Now who doesn't find *that* challenge of interest, either personally or castle-wise?

There's just something raw and sexy about a castle, whether it's the massive fortification or its true simplicity within a gargantuan interior that we humans, male and female, children and far-side-of-the-hillers, find quite mesmerizing. Thus, over the course of many centuries, the romance of the castle has remained as stalwart as its stonework, and as enchanting as many seem enchanted. A world-wide phenomenon, they're the symbol of ambition and power, stability, and safety. But above everything else, castles are the stuff of dreams and desires. Herein lies the magic and mystique of the castle.

A BRIEF HISTORY OF CASTLES

The concept of fortification, of course, is thousands of years old, beginning with the earliest tribes building protective stone and dirt barriers around their encampments. Near Dorchester, England, are the remains of what is probably one of the earliest hill-forts we can find. Its origins go back to circa 3,000 BCE, where the original campsite was comprised of a single ditch and bank. Expanded and refined over centuries, it attained its present shape by 400 BCE and now covers an area of forty-seven acres. The fortification, built by the Celts, was known as Mai Dun or Great Hill, and is known today as Maiden Castle. The complex contains outer walls surrounding an inner courtyard within a second wall which embraces a structure sitting on the high point. The embankments were created from dirt dug from ditches between the walls and

Carcassonne

embedded with the limestone rock of the area. Some rise as high as eighty feet. This compound created a protective complex for the "upper class," or ruling class, while the peons lived in huts outside the fort. Still, it was built to protect the community, while later compounds were more selective. This basic pattern was replicated for the next thousand years and proved to be very functional, as the Maiden Castle occupants lived safely until the Roman invasion in 43 CE. Their Armageddon came when the Roman army with advanced weaponry clobbered the poor rock-throwing Celts, taking over the area to build a temple and a town, and establishing what is Dorchester today.

These fortifications, later fortresses and even later, castles, were developing world-wide, though in varying forms and from whatever local materials were available, all with the purpose of repelling enemy invaders. Walls, of course, were the first and most important requisite. In 1250 BCE, the Greek city of Mycenae was surrounded with a structure thirty feet thick. At the time of Jesus, King Herod built the Masada, a fortress where 960 Jewish Zealots held out for two years against a pounding by Roman invaders. In Yucatan, Mexico, we can see a great walled city of giant stone slabs at Chichen-Itza, created fifteen hundred years ago by the Mayans. The French city of Carcassonne, built by the Romans in the first century, is perhaps the best preserved example in Europe, with the ancient walled city located outside the present one. High in the Alps above Nice, France, one can visit the walled city of St. Paul de Vence, overlooking the Mediterranean.

The form that we now define as "castle" seemed to begin in northern Europe in the tenth century, or early medieval period. Up until then, the entire territories had been stabilized by Roman rule, and later by the unification under Charlemagne, who died in 814. Norsemen came to France and established Normandy; and, so it was that the embryonic "castle concept" was brought to

Britain by the Norman, William the Conqueror, in 1066, where his persistent band of 7,000 men, using the French "motte" and "bailey" construction of fortification, whupped the 40,000 Brits after a period of four years. The Normans could assemble a hut, which they placed on a "motte" or dirt mound, and surrounded it with a "bailey" where soldiers gathered and horses were kept, all enclosed with a high picket fence. They could pull these habitats apart and tote them around, dogging the scattered British armies, until the Brits finally had had enough, and told William, "So okay, BE king." The materials' advantage was that it was of wood and light to carry, but unfortunately, it was also easy to burn. Thus, the use of native stone came into play, still using the motte and bailey form of building, but replacing the picket fence with a stone or "curtain" wall. Later, a great hall would be added where the occupants lived and life was carried on. At the same time the "keep" or high tower became the watch tower and the very last place of defense. It was around 1100 that William built one of the most well-known castles in Britain, the White Tower, or the Tower of London,

Tower of London

which we visit today to see the Crown Jewels. Seems William had a talent for construction.

Then in 1280 along came the Plantagenets with their concentric plan for castles, which simply added an outer bailey and a second wall beyond that, with a thick, sloping base, shaped much like our concrete traffic barriers today. This deflected much of what was shot at it, and could even cause cannon balls to bounce back at the shooter. By now, castles were becoming customized, with mazes to the entrance that made it hard for the enemy to find its way in, should they survive the rainstorms of arrows and the hot oil baths from above.

But of course, while castles became more and more sophisticated, so did artillery and weapons, until the castle just wouldn't suffice as the major defense in a war. By the fifteenth century, they had become merely status symbols for the wealthy. Perhaps the current paradigm of the romantic castle is Neuschwanstein, built in 1869 by the "mad"

"Motte" and "bailey"

Concentric plan

King Ludwig II of Bavaria. Built for his beloved, this dream castle of castles served as the model for Walt Disney when he created Disneyland.

CASTLES WORLD-WIDE

Those seeking European castle tours today will find a covey of them along the Loire River in France (along with many vineyards and wine caves!); and, of course, Ireland, Scotland, and England are replete with crenelated stone towers. All over the world, there are structures of defense

Neuschwanstein Castle

and safety. The pyramids of Mexico and Mayan territories are their own type of castle. Japan and China too, as well as the Middle East, hold exotic defense structures. Spain's castles are the familiar interior pattern of keep, inner wall, bailey, and outer wall, with very exciting outer designs. Wherever you go, castles are all custom-built, so the fun in finding them is that each will have its own characteristics. Should you be traveling in the near or far future, "castling" is a must. What a wonderful way to step into the past.

THE CASTLES OF COLORADO

The castles of Colorado are far from ancient, of course, but for the most part, they adhere to the code of castledom. Although their functions have adapted to modern life, the style of the castle stays the same as it has for centuries. Any remodeling of a castle is usually a clandestine integration into the original architecture, although there are some very strange anomalies in some cases. I'd like to note too that although the usual idea of a castle is the Teutonic-style of an opened-topped, crenelated turret, the French style chateau—their castle—is often topped with a round, pointed, party-hat-type roof.

The structures in this book are presented regionally. Each structure has an interesting history of concept and purpose. Many were ego extensions, like the Cherokee Castle, Falcon Castle, and Glen Eyrie. The Richthofen Castle was built partly as a bribe and partly to advertise real estate, as was Castle Marne. Others were built as a compassionate sanctuary for the sick, as was the Miramont Castle in Manitou Springs.

The champion of fulfilling a dream would be the Jim Bishop Castle near Beulah, Colorado. This castle, begun by a man of modest means in 1967, has been an on-going project ever since, and is still under construction. Working like a reincarnated pyramid builder, Bishop uses no heavy equipment but hauls each rock into place with his own hands. Here is an amazing example of how a "castle in the air" can be created with one man's focus.

Research takes one down many strange and often unrelated but enlightening paths. Exploring is absolutely the greatest joy that life can hold. And where is there a better place to explore than a castle? Come along.

There are castles in Colorado that are off-limits.

Cherokee Castle

THE CASTLE TODAY

For one brief, shining moment, one can look left while on Highway 85 just south of Sedalia and catch a glimpse of the "Camelot of Colorado," a Scottish castle capping a distant hill. A replica of the 1400s and formally known as Cherokee Ranch and Castle, it was, until recently and most famously, the home of Mildred Montigue Genevieve, called "Tweet" Kimball. A wealthy divorcee from Tennessee, Tweet bought the castle and surrounding land in 1954 as a place to raise her two sons and a breed of unique cattle. In no time at all, her gracious entertaining and good taste transformed what had been only a ranch into a unique paradigm of splendor, famous world wide for its hospitality.

The original castle and out-buildings, created from 1924 through 1926, used native stone called rhyolite, quartzite, and petrified wood for construction. The entrance hall leads into the cavernous great hall arched with hewn timbers and headed by the largest of eight stone fireplaces found throughout the home. Overlooking the great hall is the musicians' balcony, spacious enough to hold a small orchestra for the lavish parties still held below. Hand-hewn pillars are spaced along each side of the room, and the one nearest the fireplace is ornately carved at the top flange, or more properly termed the "corbel." Actually, this is the *only* pillar with an ornamented flange. The story goes that the artist who

Detail of hand-hewn mantel.

carved the pillar, as well as the stonework on the huge fireplace, had a run-in with the architect and left in a huff, abandoning his work in favor of artistic pride. However, the elegance of the furnishings, brought in by Tweet Kimball, more than compensates for the unfinished stonework. In fact, the entire castle's furnishings overshadow those in many a museum.

Each piece of furniture is a work of art in itself. The well informed docents tell the history of each piece, from the elegant brocaded sofas to the Chickering grand piano, built in 1891 and still in use. Two William and Mary Bible secretaries (desks) that pre-date Columbus stand under the cantilever of the musicians' gallery. Each has a secret drawer across the top, undetectable to the untrained eye. Here were stashed Bibles or rosaries, or perhaps a clandestine love letter.

Worthy of several minutes of study is a striking chest of ebony wood, finely inlaid with animals of ivory, depicting the fables of Aesop. The oldest piece of Tweet's glorious collection is a Grecian urn, dating back to 332 BCE. And standing at attention in a wall niche is an authentic Saxon suit of armor, caged in with spears and lances. Still, the finest furnishings found are the original oils, which include a Rembrandt, Rubens, Constable, Sir Christopher Wren, Titian, and Gainsborough, as well as many portraits of Tweet in the various stages of her life. Just outside the great hall to the south is a large porch, or terrace, used for outdoor dining. The view here is of Pike's Peak stretching west across the Front Range to Long's Peak in the north.

Just off the great hall is the dining room, with multiple windows framing the mountains to the west. On the ceiling is a handsome plaster molding in sixteenth century style. The cabinets in the room hold porcelain and hand-painted, gold-embossed china—gracious tableware that was used for the gourmet feeding of many a royal mouth.

Off the great hall is a tower with a winding staircase leading to a small library of first editions. This is a room to see only from the door-

Ebony chest with ivory Aesop figures

Bed of Charles II

way for quite obvious reasons. Many of these editions are priceless.

Another turn will lead to the upper bedrooms, where the star of the show is a bed specifically made for England's Charles II, in 1674. He even slept here (in this *bed,* not in this room, as he was dead three hundred years before the castle was built). Still the highest honor afforded a guest of the castle is to allow him or her to sleep here (with a new mattress, I'm sure.)

In 1996 Tweet established the Cherokee Ranch and Castle Foundation. She endowed it with the castle and the land, all furnishings and collections within the castle including the masterpiece paintings, and the entire cattle operation. Tweet was president of the foundation until her death in 1999. Currently the foundation, in partnership with Douglas County Open Space, provides a sheltered environment for elk, birds, and other wildlife. Its purpose is also to enhance cultural life in

Colorado and provide educational opportunities, particularly regarding our western heritage, wildlife and the arts. It is also very important to repeat that the castle and grounds are open space for *wildlife*, but not for people. Hiking, camping, and activities are not allowed here, and entrance to the castle and its grounds must first be requested.

Dining room with groined ceiling

4   Teas and tours are held on the weekends as well as many educational seminars, and the castle also offers a spectacular and memorable venue for weddings or special parties if planned ahead.

HISTORY OF THE CASTLE

The castle itself was originally commissioned in 1924 by Denver real estate tycoon Charles A. Johnson and his wife Alice, who sought out Burnham Hoyt, a Denver architect of renown, to do their design. Hoyt designed it in the Scottish style circa 1450, complete with turrets and a tower, and used native stone actually quarried on the

Well house

Courtyard and stable from tower.

property. Thirty masons, originally from Cornwall, England, spent two years hand-hewing the stones for this magnificent structure. What started out to be a modest dwelling grew over the two years until it finally contained twenty-six rooms sprawling to some 10,000 square feet. Additionally, a two-story horse barn and two well houses were built. The barn, built by Hoyt, is wood frame with a game

The Johnson stone house, called "Chickamauga."

room above the livery. The octagonal well houses are stone and still function.

The owner, Charles Johnson, was nearing retirement when he had the castle built. He had come to Denver as a young man, and had befriended the eccentric but genuine Baron von Winkler. This odd character had had the foresight to buy land on the plains east of Denver that he was developing as the village known as Park Hill. As one of von Winkler's few friends, Johnson was asked to handle the von Winkler estate after his death in 1898, and it was the sale of property of the Park Hill Ranch that made Johnson a very rich man.

Johnson himself must have been quite a unique fellow. His previous palatial home in Park Hill had been titled "The Hut," a tongue-in-cheek response to the lesser dwellings around, often referred to as "mansions." Widowed by age fifty, he left his business to drive for the Ambulance Corps in France during World War I. Here he met his second wife, Alice, whom he married in 1920.

For thirty years, the Johnsons lived on their 2,380 acres, in their stone castle heated by a coal furnace. The land had been bought from the Flower family who had originally homesteaded the property in 1894. Several buildings from the original homestead are still on the property. The Johnson stone house, called "Chickamauga," is now used to accommodate employees, and wooden additions made to the original house now house ranch workers.

Down the hill from the Flower property was the Blunt Homestead filed in 1868, with the very hill being named Blunt Mountain. The family had lived and farmed here on 1,550 acres for eighty-one years

when Tweet Kimball bought the property, house, and barns, and incorporated them into her Cherokee Ranch, along with three other properties. Proudly elegant, the Blunt house still stands and was used for many years as a home for the ranch foreman. It speaks well for the Blunt's construction abilities, and the Flowers as well. The Brazos and Alamo barns are listed on the National List of Historic Places, and are still in use, both as meeting areas and for storage.

Currently, the Blunt house is being renovated and will be put to use as an education or meeting facility. It also will be used to give school children a close-up experience with animals and their care.

TWEET KIMBALL

When Tweet Kimball bought the castle and adjoining land in 1954, she renamed the area Cherokee Mountain after the Native American tribe in her state of Tennessee. She updated the heating and entertained lavishly, hosting distinguished visitors from all corners of the world. It is said that Tweet ranched in cowboy boots by day and entertained royally, quite literally and often *with* royalty, in the evenings. Tweet's many important friends and guests included Prince Bernhardt of the Netherlands, Britain's Princess

Tweet's bedroom, but now a dressing room for brides.

Anne, the crown prince of Nepal, Princess Alexandra, cousin to Elizabeth II, and many lesser lords and ladies, as well as associates from the ranching and horse communities.

A true individualist, "Tweet" Kimball had left the social life in Tennessee to move to Colorado, where she hunkered down in a castle with her two young sons and raised a breed of cattle that she was told wouldn't survive the Colorado winters.

The herd of Santa Gertrudis had been bred by the Kings Ranch in Texas, crossing Brahma cattle with short horns. In 1955, Tweet Kimball bought twenty-nine cows and two bulls and, against all advice, had them shipped to her ranch in Colorado. Cattlemen predicted the animals wouldn't survive the cold winters, and heck, what

Top: Memorial Garden; below: garden gate

was a woman doing breeding cattle anyway? History proved *her* right. The cattle thrived, and she became a legend.

This "legend" was born in Chattanooga, Tennessee, daughter of a West Pointer, Colonel Richard H. Kimball. Tweet's nickname was established before her birth by her artistic father, who sent letters home to his wife adorned with cute characters called "Tweets." Raised as a society debutant, she originally married Merritt Ruddock, later a member of the U.S. diplomatic corps (the first of four husbands) and with whom she adopted her two sons. Upon divorcing many years later, she told a reporter in 1996 that "When I divorced him, he said I'd probably go back to Tennessee and talk about him. He said, 'If you'll buy property west of the Mississippi, I'll help you.'" It was this win-win situation that kept her out of Tennessee and allowed her to follow her dream of ranching.

As an avid equestrian and superb rider, she hosted a yearly party for the Arapahoe Hunt Club at Cherokee, and spent years on the board of the National Western Stock Show. The Birds of Prey Foundation, an organization for injured raptors, was a major interest of hers. After many years, she is still listed as Director at Large. In 1997, she was given the Dana Crawford Award as someone prominent in the preservation of Colorado history. One of her final acts was to endow her possessions in perpetuity and to align her foundation with that of the Douglas County Open Space, giving Cherokee Mountain a conservation easement.

The eclectic Tweet also loved fine art, and gave to the acquisition fund for the Denver Art Museum, also serving on the board there for many years.

Atop a hill to your right as you drive up to the castle is the Memorial Garden, built by Tweet's admirers and her final resting place since 1999. The massive carved stone archway into the garden is sometimes used as a location for wedding ceremonies. Its heavy iron gates were rescued from her family home in Chattanooga before it was bulldozed to make way for a highway.

SCANDAL

One wonders just what silence Ruddock was buying when he offered to sponsor his wife in anything she wanted, as long as she moved far from

her original home. Rumor has it that he was the immediate deputy of the CIA's Frank Wisner, the overseer of Nazi recruitment by the agency immediately after World War II. Researching Wisner on the Internet, one finds a portrait of a power-driven and influential member of a government agency involved in a variety of unscrupulous manipulation. Taking Tweet's remark as an accurate quote, that the castle was actually a bribe, it would seem that Tweet was aware of the inner workings of the CIA and that her husband had been involved. Still, her good works certainly put a high shine on the lady, and there is no doubt that she is one of the major legends of Colorado.

ACCESS

Teas may be scheduled for Wednesday afternoons. Tours are conducted on Wednesdays, Thursdays, and Saturdays, but any appointments must be made ahead of time. Cherokee also is a place for weddings, educational or corporate events, and cultural performances. (See Events chart.) Call (303) 688-5555 or log onto www.cherokeeranch.org.

DIRECTIONS: U.S. 85 west off I-25 or down Santa Fe from Littleton toward Castle Rock. Turn north onto Daniels Park Road and drive one mile to the stone pillar gate. Turn left and take the dirt road for two more miles to the castle. Please do not go unannounced.

Dunafon Castle

THE CASTLE TODAY

Hidden below the winding road along Bear Creek two miles above Idledale is a fairy tale castle in the idyllic surrounds of ponds, a river, lawns, and guardian trees. Backed up against a mountain, the sturdy grey stone structure faces the now swollen waters, turret foremost, with the castle's two levels both available from the ground level. Its classic design at first seems Greek, but is actually Gaelic. (Castles of this type have been found in many areas of the world due to the subsequent migration of people for religious and economic reasons.) It was constructed in the 1930s with stones gathered from the land to build a round keep, the hefty walls enclosing fourteen rooms, two towers, the carriage house, and the upstairs living quarters. Stone walls also buttress a terrace, and house the newly restored generators. Two massive bridges of stone, one fording the trout pond, and another spanning the river itself—create a picture of permanence.

It's a setting of serenity, here on the lawn, with the quiet castle behind, the ponds at my feet, a massive waterwheel one hundred yards away against a stone wall, and the single sound coming from the river, grumbling at the rocks in its path. The complex is truly a dream come true, and, I find, for a growing number of people.

Mike Dunafon and Debbie Matthews came across this property in 2004. It was seventeen acres encased in underbrush and trash, ponds dense

Awaiting the wedding party

The great hall, previously an eight-car garage

with muck and algae, and its buildings nearly obliterated in overgrowth. Mike and Debbie bought the property and then contacted a friend who ran a program called Step 13, a self-help program for homeless drug addicts. The friend, Bob Coté, trucked in thirty strong and willing men, and with their help and commitment, the castle and grounds have been rehabbed into its current state of tranquility and contentment.

Functionally the castle is a private residence but is occasionally used for gala weddings and celebrations. The front of the castle faces the river on the lower level. What was once a carriage house and later an eight-car garage now serves as a great hall, opening onto a large stone patio covered by a tent. The great hall itself has the requisite welcoming fireplace, and three walls are hand painted with scenes of Colorado. This room can seat seventy-five guests, and an equal number can be seated

Ten-foot wide over-shot waterwheel provides electricity.

out on the patio, which overlooks the lawn and three tiers of trout ponds. The focal point of the patio is a wrought iron gazebo with a flaming oil lamp chandelier—a romantic transition into the past. Off the great hall and several steps down is a basement area called "the dungeon," which is

Wrought iron gazebo with flaming oil lamp chandelier.

Semi-spiral staircase from upper level and private quarters.

Wine cellar

One of the generators supplying power to the castle.

actually a superb area for the three ten-foot long banquet tables, end-to-end, capable of seating over two dozen people. The long, up-sloped hall going from the great hall into the castle is punctuated by a restroom on one side and a wine cellar at the end, before making a right turn into a living room area. From there, a semi-spiral staircase leads to the upper level and private quarters.

Although the elegance of the past has been restored, the castle is still a work in progress. A four-hundred-foot-long tunnel, large enough for a man to walk in, originally was the pipeline carrying water from a dam on Bear Creek to the powerhouse to run the generators. This tunnel-pipeline and the generators are now being restored and will soon function as they originally did, supplying all the power needed for the castle. A small railway, actually a replica of a mining train that once carted ore and people around the property is also being resurrected.

All work now in progress on the property is done by men in the Step 13 program and Mike Dunafon himself. The ambiance of the castle seems to work well for everyone, as the rate of success of Step 13 is 38 percent, as compared to an estimated 5 percent in government programs. It's the *real* magic of accomplishment and responsibility.

Weddings and celebrations are held at the castle by appointment. There are several venues. In addition to the lower area with its in-and-out access to the lawn and ponds, the castle offers two upper rooftops of 3,600 square feet for dining or dancing under the stars. They too can be tented,

The castle as seen from the gazebo

and overlook the trout ponds and river. For nighttime atmosphere, the roof is ringed with unique castle lights, and the view is of the spectacularly lit lawn area starring the gazebo and its fiery candelabra.

Winter too, is celebrated here, with snowshoeing, horse-drawn sleigh rides, ice-skating, ice-fishing, and dinner served before the roaring fire in the great hall.

The owners calculate their cost, pass it on to the clients and ask for an additional donation for one of three charities, which they will then match. Those charities are Step 13, the Central City Opera Company, and the Glendale Y.M.C.A. To arrange for a tour, call 720-528-4023.

HISTORY OF THE CASTLE

I'd say that Marcus C. Wright was a man who took his work home with him. Owner and operator of an engineering and manufacturing business in Denver in the 1930s and 40s, Wright bought 1,240 acres in the canyon of Bear Creek and built himself a castle from the local rock near the banks of the river. He began in 1929, working part-time and on weekends with his workmen over a period of nearly twelve years. Completed in 1941 and christened Castle Springs Ranch, it was indeed a relic of the past on the exterior, built of stone with the requisite towers and crenelation, but internally it was as avant garde as the knowledgeable Wright could make it. Stones were held together

Finished castle after 1941

with reinforced concrete, making it both fireproof and low maintenance. Hardware and doorknobs throughout were fashioned in the shape of maple leaves. The double-paned windows pivoted open on a central bar like the wings of a butterfly. The kitchen was stainless steel from dishwasher to the range, and it even had an incinerator.

Electricity was quite the passion of Wright's life. He built a miniature electric railroad to surround the property, taking visitors on a spectacular half-mile ride to view his trout ponds and surrounding forests. Best of all, the electricity was free, since it was generated by two hydroelectric plants that he created. One was directly connected to a small turbine waterwheel, while the larger plant was fed by a ten-foot wide over-shot waterwheel situated on the upper trout pond, adding a very scenic focal point to the landscape. Both plants were housed in the powerhouse, which itself was fireproof, encased in reinforced concrete and surrounded by stone.

Internalizing his exterior castle design, Wright placed 102 two interior lights—each fixture a miniature castle—throughout the castle as well as along the roof. The hand-fashioned light fixtures may have been one of the highest expenditures of the building.

Wright lived a turbulent life in his castle from 1941 until he died in 1958. (It's reported that Mrs. Wright never did move in, and the castle went into trust upon his death.) Twelve years later, in 1970, it was purchased by William M. Barnes and his wife, Tamsin, and included only seventeen surrounding acres. In the interim, the castle, owned by a bank, had been empty for the greater period of time. However, it had at times been rented out, and even had a history of being a "cat house" and a place of gambling.

The Barnes' purchased a major fixer-upper. The roof leaked, only 30 percent of the electrical wiring worked, the powerhouse was inoperable, and the grounds were totally overgrown with black willow and scrub trees, which were choking up the trout ponds and flower beds. After clearing out the underbrush, the Barnes' planted fruit trees to add color. Concrete bridges were constructed over the moats and the ponds cleared for fish. Although the train track was still there, the cars were all gone. Barnes found a used diesel engine at an amusement park that he purchased, adding one little car that could hold passengers for a ride around the grounds.

Inside the castle, the once-carriage house on the lower level became an entertainment room. It was equipped with full-size gambling equipment including a crap table, a wheel of fortune, and a blackjack table, and outside on the patio, a swimming pool. Barnes also added a twenty-five foot mechanized, fire-breathing dragon to the top of the building to welcome visitors. Up the hall from the game room the once-reception room became a library, completely lined from floor to ceiling with bookshelves. On the upper level, the remodeled kitchen was enlarged by removing the wall to

Miniature castle light fixtures

the hall, and a Franklin stove was installed in place of the incinerator.

The Barnes' lived there for thirty years, raising their four daughters until tragedy struck. In 1999, Bill Barnes along with wife, Tamsin, and daughter Paula, were on Egypt Air flight 990 out of JFK Airport, when it crashed less than an hour after take-off, killing everyone on board. No reason has ever been found for the tragic crash. Egypt Air still holds the case open.

One daughter, Lisa, stayed in the castle until 2004, when it was sold to Mike Dunafon and Debbie Matthews. Shades of the Brothers Grimm.

In 2004, the couple came across the property choked with under- and over-growth so severe that even finding their Sleeping Beauty—the castle itself—was a problem. Lucky for all, Dunafon is a visionary, and could see beneath the massive problems of decay and neglect. Manpower provided by Step 13 immediately dug in, clearing brush, hauling trash and garbage, ripping out the old carpets and repairing the walls. They painted the high ceilings and interior, and even hand-carved furniture for the castle. In a classic win-win situation, the castle emerged from its casing of trash and litter while the men of Step 13 gained confidence and pride in their work.

Dunafon poured over old blueprints and photographs and interviewed surviving members of the previous owners. His plan was to restore the castle, rather than just build and remodel. The biggest challenge was the power plant, knee-deep in muck and trash. Dunafon hired engineer R.A. "Skip" Campbell, who was an expert on the old type of electrical and plumbing that had been used throughout the castle. With dirt and grime sanded off the old generator wheel, the name "Ralph" could be seen on the wheel. In a bizarre coincidence, Ralph, creator of the wheel, turned out to be Skip's great uncle. And oddly again, Skip's first name is Ralph. Ralph Campbell, creator and re-creator of the generator.

Within the past three years, the castle, grounds, and ponds have been rescued, and are now ready for company. Somehow, more than any other castle, this one seems to be not a link to the past, but perhaps more of a gateway.

Children's treehouse

MIKE DUNAFON

Other chapters are about pioneers, and this one is also, with the difference that he is still here, and history is in the making.

Mike Dunafon is a Colorado native, born in Golden in 1954 and currently the Mayor Pro-Tem of Glendale. Strongly influenced by his father and uncle who were ranchers and rodeo riders, young Mike learned that it was reliability and responsibility that were the strong threads in the fabric of life. Football was also a strong influence in his life. Playing from the time he was in junior high until he was with the Denver Broncos, Mike learned teamwork, but with the goal of winning, almost at any cost. Then, propitiously, he was introduced to the

game of rugby, where he found what he terms "competitive cooperation"—a game where your opponent is also respected and treated as a friend, and though winning is a goal, the emphasis is on teamwork and sportsmanship. Games are practices for living, and the rugby philosophy seemed much the better approach. Now Mike and Debbie are actively supporting the Y.M.C.A. in Glendale, and are building a rugby field there with hopes of promoting the competitive cooperative spirit in their own community. They've also stocked the trout ponds at the castle, and have a program of catch-and-release for disadvantaged children to learn fishing.

Debbie Matthews sang with Antonia Brico's Classic Choral, and opera is a second interest.

Castle wall construction

Second floor layout and rebar construction

Carriage House construction

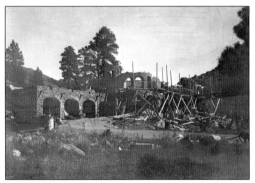

Castle framework

Castle arches in place

Powerhouse and waterwheel

South wall beginning rock work

Cement mixer

Rock crusher

Bridge under construction. Marcus Wright and children

Water diversion with the foreman

Building rock wall around dam

Overflow from Pond One

Finished bridge

View of castle and water wheel from Pond Three

Some of the funds from castle programs go to sponsor talented young singers who could use a financial leg up.

The primary focus however, is on the Step 13 program, founded twenty-three years ago by Bob Coté, a one-time addict himself. Applicants must apply for help and not have a history of child abuse or violence. They sign an agreement to further their own education at whatever level they may be and must take a course called "Your Credit Counts," to develop financial responsibility. The average time for completing the program is eighteen months, and the graduates have an impressive 38 percent success rate. The program is not federally funded, and although that creates difficulties in funding somewhat, it also avoids reels of red tape and bureaucratic interference. Funding then, relies on outside sources like Dunafon Castle to employ the men, and the program itself owns several businesses detailing cars and trucks, and also the service of silkscreen/embroidery/engraving.

Mike Dunafon is a paradox of sorts. Raised in a smoky atmosphere of heavy testosterone, he graduated from college with a Fine Arts degree and spends his energy in a quest to make life better for the people around him, both children and floundering adults. His leisure time is spent writing poetry and songs for his guitar.

SCANDAL

There are two issues here: the first is that sometime between Wright's death and Barnes' acquisition, the castle was at one time a brothel and gambling casino. The second issue is more serious. The plane crash that killed three of the Barnes family has never been properly explained, and the investigation of the crash is still open.

HAUNTED

With its history, it would be surprising if the castle did *not* have spirits. Lisa Barnes, who lived there as a child, believes the castle is truly an entity—very alive itself, with its energy deriving from the structure being made of solid rock, with materials all from the surrounding area. Wright, the man who actually created the castle, was building his own dream—certainly a positive beginning. And the rock is granite, Lisa adds, which vibrates at a very low frequency and has accumulated its history over time, both positive and negative.

Lisa is a Sensitive, or Medium, and has been aware of a multitude of spirits around the castle. As a child, she often heard footsteps along the long hallway from the garage into the house, though no one visible was there. In fact, guests staying in the lower bedrooms adjacent to the hall, complained to her parents about the noise that disturbed their sleeping. Another annoyance was a spirit dog whose nails clicked on the terrazzo floor and whose panting would awaken Lisa.

Following the airplane crash, the castle was on the market for four years, with several interested buyers. But Lisa found it disturbing that these potential owners were interested in the land only, and planned to scrap the castle and rebuild. Then Dunafon and Matthews found the estate,

and it was the castle that they wanted, and wished to restore. Soon after, Lisa encountered the spirit of her mother who assured her that they were the right people to own it.

I feel an aura of enchantment. Many, I'm sure, will be skeptical. But my private opinion is that the Dunafon Castle is unlike any other castle I've encountered.

ACCESS

Located 2.5 miles out of Idledale toward Kittredge, the castle and grounds are accessible only by appointment. To arrange for a tour or to learn about using it for an event, call 303-378-1533.

Information on the web is at www.dunafoncastle.com.

DENVER AREA

Castle Marne

THE CASTLE TODAY

Castle Marne perches on an inner city Denver lot rather than a grand estate, making it an anomaly in this book. Originally built for a real estate entrepreneur as a show home, today it is a Victorian bed and breakfast with the interior faithfully replicated from period photographs. Marne is castle-*like*, and quite exciting to come across while in the Capitol Hill section of Denver. However, its importance here is its connection to one of Denver's most important and flamboyant architects.

Designed in 1889 by famous Denver architect William Lang, Castle Marne certainly has some of the castle requisites: a "keep" and stone structure, though "castle" was not its original designation. Built of hand-hewn native rhyolite, it is of the Richardson-Romanesque style with massive stone walls, eyebrow dormers, squat towers and rounded arches. The interior is a voyage back in time. Owners Diane and Jim Peiker bought the structure in the late 1980s—a vandalized, flood-damaged building with a beautiful face—and using photographs of the original interior, have reestablished its grandeur.

An imposing foyer has its own ornately carved fireplace. Above the mantel is a round, beveled mirror, flat at the bottom, so, shaped much like a flat tire. This, I learned, was a signature of a Lang structure that he particularly favored. The grand staircase is separated from the foyer by a

Eyebrow dormers over the windows

Grand staircase

The parlor, and above, hand-painted frieze

swooping horseshoe opening surrounded by Victorian-age bric-a-brac in golden oak. Restoration of this area was almost a miracle, as the water from broken pipes had torturously twisted and warped the rounded edging as well as part of the decorative wall. The Peikers were lucky to have a devoted relative who was a cabinet maker, and willing to spend some thousand hours steaming, gluing, and teasing the wood back into its original shape.

Up the staircase is a *pièce de résistance*—a stunning "peacock" window of both stained and beveled glass, and some six feet in diameter, lighting up the landing. It too, has the signature flat-bottomed circle.

The parlor, off to the right of the entry, has been restored to its original splendor. An artist took over six months to recreate the decorative frieze, or horizontal wide band near the ceiling, pictured in photographs of the original room. In fact, the Peikers have attempted to even replicate the furnishings of the age, as evidenced by a charming stereopticon on the coffee table with dozens of old photos for the viewer. Inset in an intricately carved mantel of deep mahogany, two serpent-looking dolphins, historically harbingers of welcome and good luck, use their tails to hold up carved baskets on each end above the massive fireplace. Below the dolphins is the face of the Green Man, the Celtic consort of Mother Earth, with facial hair of leaves. He guarantees spring and the renewal of the earth, and can even be found carved in the ancient Christian cathedrals in Europe.

Victorian dining room and solarium with hand-painted flowers on ceiling

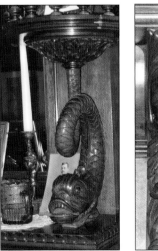

The southwest corner of the parlor is the interior of the Queen Anne tower, a green oasis flooded with light and a wonderful nook for reading or working on the current resident jigsaw puzzle. The sunny conservatory on the southeast end is an addition to the original building and overlooks the Victorian garden. Note the Palladian window facing south. Lang was experimenting here with several window forms.

Straight ahead as you pass through the entry is the dining room, paneled in the original quarter-sawn oak, and papered with the actual original Lincrusta wallcovering from England. Further authenticity is provided by the hand-painted flowers around the oval in the ceiling and along the top of the wall above the picture molding. Originally flowers of Asia, the Peikers replaced them with the flowers of Colorado. Dining areas were often solariums, or at least, suggestions of them. The large table, set with Victorian-age china, and all the fussiness of the age, makes one feel very important and welcome.

Up the grand staircase out of the foyer, I walk straight into the Presidential Suite, the most glamorous of accommodations, with three rooms of

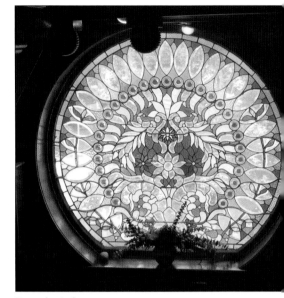

Peacock window

comfort that Victorians never dreamed of. There's even a balcony looking west to see city lights, and beyond that, snow-covered peaks. Directly above, on the third level, is the John Mason Suite, named after the second owner and a world-renown naturalist. This modern, sunlit room embodies the challenges faced by the Peikers, and is a triumph of their reconstruction. Here is the epitome of an elegant suite complete with its own private spa, but flavored in Victorian. Delicious. Down the hall here and on the third floor you'll find smaller rooms, but all are intriguing bowers decked in florals and lace, soft cushions, and vintage furnishings.

All in all, there are nine guest rooms here, two of which are suites and several equipped with their own Jacuzzis and spas. A gourmet breakfast is included in the price, as is the formal tea held each afternoon from 4:30 P.M. until 6:00 P.M.

Some of John T. Mason's butterflies

Located on Race Street at the corner of Sixteenth Avenue, The Marne is convenient to all the downtown attractions, is listed on the National Register of Historic Structures, and is a Denver Landmark Building.

HISTORY OF THE CASTLE

The castle was originally built for Wilbur S. Raymond, a real estate investor who had purchased an entire section of land outside the smoke and bustle of downtown Denver. He chose the highest point on a hilltop and hired Denver's top architect, William Lang, to build what would be his "show home" for a planned community. Money seemed to be no object, as this structure and the land cost an estimated $55,000, at least twice what Lang's far better known "Molly Brown House" had cost. The Raymond home was truly opulent, with a grand foyer of quarter-sawn oak leading to formal parlor and dining area, and the great oak staircase to many bedrooms as well as a Grand Ballroom on the third level.

It seems to have been an investment based on a solid theory, but the timing was poor, if not calamitous. A recession was creeping in nationwide, and although the location for upper-income housing was superb, the Denver real estate market went from soft to soggy. Raymond had taken a gamble, borrowing heavily to finance his dream home. He and his family had lived in the house barely a year before it was repossessed by creditors.

Colonel James H. Platt purchased the home in 1890 from the bank. Platt was a veteran of the

Civil War and had served in President Grant's cabinet after his election as a congressional representative from Virginia for six terms. In 1885, after selling out his percentage of a business he owned with John D. Rockefeller, the colonel moved to Denver to create the Denver Paper Mills Company. Here he built a gigantic paper mill, originally at West Louisiana and Jason streets, at an estimated cost of $570,000. When completed, it was the largest building in Colorado. Platt and his wife lived in the Raymond house from 1891 until his drowning under mysterious circumstances during a fishing trip in 1894. Denver has commemorated

this pioneer, naming a park after him. (Note that the river "Platte" is spelled with an "E," and is Spanish for "flat." No relationship here.)

A memorial to the next owner still hangs in the upstairs hall outside the Presidential Suite. John T. Mason, who bought the home in 1895, was a world-famous lepidopterist and a fabulous butterfly collection is displayed at the top of the staircase. Mason was founder and the first curator of Denver's Museum of Natural History, now the Museum of Nature and Science. Portions of his vast collection of over 40,000 butterflies and moths were displayed in the ballroom until it was donated to the museum in 1928 at the time of his death. The name of John T. Mason is permanently chiseled in the marble wall of the Greek Theatre in Denver's Civic Center, along with other city benefactors.

Life has its ups and downs, and so do castles. Purchased in 1918 by the widow Adele Van Cise, along with her son, Philip, the mansion was converted into apartments. Mrs. Van Cise actually moved some outside walls of the castle to establish areas compatible to multiple units. Rooms were subdivided and walls added to accommodate separate living quarters. They were the first to call the structure "The Marne," possibly because Philip had fought in the Battle of the Marne in World War I. Philip Van Cise was a prominent Denver attorney, representing the *Rocky Mountain News* during the famous *Denver Post*/Fred Bonfils scandal and trial. As district attorney for Denver, he mounted a war against gambling, prostitution, organized crime, and the Ku Klux Klan.

Adele Van Cise lived at The Marne until her death in 1937, and the next owner, Mr. Lyle Holland, maintained the apartments through the war years, and until his death in 1974.

Speculators came and went for the next several years. Louise and Richard Dice took possession in 1976 with the goal of creating three condo units—one per floor. This was a failed enterprise. Then from 1979 through 1982, the building served as a processing center for parolees from state penal institutions. All walls, carpet, and surroundings were done in drab shades of regulation gray, creating a pretty grim interior.

For several years after, the castle stood vacant. A group of doctors wanted to convert it into offices, but found insufficient space for parking. A lawyers' group owned it and probably for the same reason, never took occupancy. Abandoned, the castle suffered heavy damage from broken water pipes and inevitable vandalism. But its sorry state put the castle into a price bracket that the Peikers could afford.

Jim and Diane Peiker both come from Denver families of pioneer stock. Looking for a location to start a bed and breakfast, they came across the deserted hulk in 1988. Digging through thick layers of wallpaper and stripping paint off woodwork, they labored along with the best professional craftsmen available to reproduce the images in photos they found, sometimes in the attic and often in the library. Miraculously, the castle was opened one year later and now has become an authentic time tunnel back to the age of Victoria.

WILLIAM LANG

You're forgiven for bragging if your beautiful old Denver home was designed by William Lang. Lang was Denver's most popular and prolific architect in the decade from 1883 to 1893, an era of the city's coming-of-age. Denver was segueing from a frontier town beleaguered by Indians and drunken miners, to an industrial center connected to the rest of the country by rail lines and communication. She was becoming a city, and, feeling her oats, was determined to create herself in solid, permanent brick and stone. Enter the master of stonework, William Lang.

Born in the midwest in 1846, Lang seemed to have tip-toed out of oblivion into the architectural community from the midwest, and apparently was self-taught. Arriving in Denver in 1885, he frenetically set to work designing anything anyone was willing to hire him for, from "chicken coops to cathedrals," according to Lang expert, Dr. Charles O. Brantigan. Lang's name first appears in the city directory as an architect in 1886, corresponding with his formation of a partnership with Marshall R. Pugh. While Lang handled the design, Pugh was the engineer.

In 1888, A. M. Ghost, a real estate man from Nebraska, became Lang's landlord, and in this same year, Lang began his meteoric rise. By 1889,

Lang and Pugh had a suite of rooms in the Ghost Block at Seventeenth and Champa streets, a building Lang had designed. (This building, Lang's only commercial structure in Denver, was moved into storage, stone by stone, with each stone numbered, around 1980. Stored for ten years, it was reconstructed at its present location at Nineteenth and Stout streets around 1990.)

Between the years of 1888 and 1893, Lang's work with stone was his signature on many mansions of Capitol Hill. Although strongly influenced by the Richardsonian and the Romanesque styles, Lang picked and chose his motifs, expanding and shrinking, adding and inflating, creating a unique style until it is obvious that Denver's most eclectic stone homes are indeed those of Lang, the mix-master. Embellishing the already elaborate Richardsonian style, he would add gargoyles, stones varying in color and texture, and columns of contrasting styles. Antithetical to these basically Victorian homes were the open, light-flooded interiors. The genius of Lang is that despite this strange mélange of style, his buildings somehow came together. It is very possible that it was the lack of formal training that allowed Lang an open mind to freely choose from various architectural styles. His art was his ability to tastefully blend.

Lang became a founding member of the Colorado Chapter of the American Institute of Architects in 1892, but at the same time, life was becoming difficult. Early in 1893, judgments against him were being served, and properties he held were going into foreclosure due to the severe recession. The Lang family's horse, road wagon,

Fireplace and flat-bottomed mirror in entry.

recall his own birthday, let alone his address. Caring for him must have been a nearly impossible task. In August of 1897, he wandered from his brother's home, and ended up in Morris, Illinois. Arrested as a vagrant and fined three dollars, which he didn't have, he was taken to jail. The jailor, disgusted with his filth, took him to the edge of town and released him, where, disoriented, he followed the train tracks toward Marseilles. He was hit by the morning train and killed instantly. Only because of the charity of the Grand Army of the Republic was he given a decent burial in Marseilles. They stepped forth when there was no response from anywhere else. It was a tragic and miserable ending for a Denver artist and pioneer.

Still, the story doesn't end there. In 1980, William Lang was honored posthumously by Historic Denver for "contributing to energy conservation by utilizing design features that created comfortable living environments without the use of energy-consuming devices." Lang was indeed a pioneer.

A TOUR OF LANG HOMES

A drive through the core of Denver can be like an Easter egg hunt, with Lang's glorious stone buildings the prize. I'll list below those given status by the Denver Historical Society, many of which are constructed with his intricate stonework. Notice that many of these homes were built in clusters, and were meant to compliment each other. So, though they may be similar, they are not replications but were built more as a set.

and harness were seized for nonpayment of a feed bill, and their furniture was repossessed. Even his wife's savings, which had been poured into their home, were lost with the foreclosure of the house. With all their material wealth gone, the couple was still being harassed even though their only possessions were the clothes on their backs. Hiring a lawyer was impossible without funds. With all the pressure, their minds, particularly William's, began to weaken.

In 1895, Lang suffered a complete collapse and was treated for insomnia, impaired memory, and mental weakness, with depression leading to a progressive dementia. No alcohol was involved in his problems, as was reported elsewhere.

His wife, Delia, stayed on with a relative in Denver while Lang was discharged to the care of his brother in Englewood, Illinois. (It is recorded that Delia died in November of 1913.) Lang was showing severe signs of dementia, not able to even

Most famous of his structures is the *Molly Brown House* with its stone lions at the entrance. At *1340 Pennsylvania*, it is a flamboyant Queen Anne, elegant in style with Romanesque strength and Victorian detail. It's also a very interesting and successful museum, but actually quite plain in design compared to Castle Marne.

One block away is the castle-like *Dunning-Benedict Mansion at 1200 Pennsylvania*, also of the Richardson Romanesque style with circular and angled towers.

Several blocks to the west is *St. Mark's Parish Church at 1160 Lincoln*, a Victorian Gothic originally with a crenulated bell tower, now gone but not forgotten.

Drive north and east to *2105 Lafayette Street* to the *Foster LeNeve Cathcart House*, a Queen Anne-style with ornate carvings and moldings in stone.

The *Washington Street Houses* are all in the same block, at *1624, 1625* and *1648*, and are solid, rusticated stone. The Lang residence was at *1638*.

At *1600 Ogden Street* is the *Bailey Mansion*, a generous turreted Queen Anne constructed of rhyolite and sandstone.

Several blocks east again will find you at *Castle Marne, 1572 Race Street*. In fact, most of the homes on the east side of that block were designed by Lang.

At *1532 Emerson Street*, find the wonderful *"Gargoyle House."*

Much of the *1400 block of Vine Street*, including *1411* and the *Tedford House at 1415 Vine* are of Lang's design.

Lang also built numerous homes of lesser stature, and some 150 homes in the Baker area alone are attributed to him, as well as many in Montclair and other outlying suburbs. The most extensive research on Lang, done by Doctor Charles Brantigan, estimates that in Lang's relatively short career, he designed more than 250 homes and other buildings.

SCANDAL

The most scandalous part of this Lang doctrine was Denver's lack of response to his announced death. Upon discovering Lang's identity and realizing his past stature as an architect in Denver, the sheriff in Marseilles ran ads in *The Denver Post* to find someone who would claim the body or sponsor a decent funeral. No one responded, and only through the grace of the Grand Army of the Republic did that occur.

ACCESS

The Castle Marne is a bed and breakfast and available all year round, with an almost eerie feeling of the past. Downtown Denver, the zoo, art museum, and City Park are almost within walking distance, and the location is superb for those who wish to enjoy the city. A complete gourmet breakfast is served every morning, and complimentary tea, coffee, or soft drink on the veranda in the evening. For reservations, call 303-331-0621, or 1-800-92-MARNE (62763).

DIRECTIONS: The Castle Marne is located at 1572 Race street, one block north of Colfax Avenue and sixteen blocks east of Broadway.

DENVER AREA

Richthofen Castle

When Jerry Priddy says his home is his castle, he's being quite literal. Priddy, his wife Esther, and their family have called Richthofen Castle their home for the past twenty-three years after Fate seemed to put it in their path. As antique dealers and owners of the auction house Estate Auction, the Priddys first acquired the contents of the castle in 1976 following the death of a previous owner. In 1984, several years and several owners later, the castle, with its history of vacancy and vandalism, went on the market as a "fixer-upper." Perhaps it seemed like a good place for the furniture, and the Priddys bravely bought it.

Only the floors were in good shape, according to Esther. They first replaced the necessities of a new boiler and furnace and updated the electrical system and water heaters. Gates hung on sprung hinges, doors wouldn't close, windows were broken, and all the chandeliers were smashed. Replacing the glass and repairing or replacing other damage, they refinished the oak-paneled entry halls and restored the hand-tooled leather walls. Over the years, Jerry, a pilot once himself, has collected memorabilia of the famous German fighter pilot, Manfred von Richthofen, nephew of the castle builder and of Snoopy fame. In his basement, he has created the Red Baron Pub, complete with mannequins in appropriate dress. The *pièce de résistance* of his collection is a replica of the Red

Baron's plane in the yard, a full-scale version of his Fokker DR-1 triplane, in "German red," complete with Iron Cross markings.

It took many years and many dollars, but restoration has been completed, and three generations of Priddys have grown up in the castle, or enjoyed it on holidays. And the grateful castle has seemed to quiet its ghosts in gratitude, despite its turbulent past.

It's unfortunate that such a fascinating and beautiful building cannot be seen by the public, although the Priddys have tried. Perfect for historic tours with a large area to park cars, they proposed the idea several years ago, but were shouted down by vigorous neighborhood opposition, and at the last minute, the rezoning was denied. Thus, the castle seems destined to be a private home, and is now on the market for $3.5 million, since the Priddy clan has grown up and gone. A couple more million will buy the furnishings as well.

HISTORY OF THE CASTLE

Here is a castle of romance, built "all for the love of a lady." Constructed on a large plot of land, then fifteen miles outside the city of Denver, it was the capstone in Baron Walter von Richthofen's plan to win the heart of divorcee, Mrs. Louise Ferguson Davies. And to add to the ante, the baron promised to create an elegant neighborhood around the castle as he sold off pieces of his large property to the wealthy, thus providing a lavish lifestyle for himself and his intended. He did indeed win his lady, marrying her in 1887, the same year he finished the castle. Starkly alone, it stood on the

Face of Barbarossa, King Frederick I of Germany.

plains, a Romanesque style structure of native rhyolite stone, brusquely Germanic and fashioned after the original Richthofen Castle in Germany. High above the front entrance he had carved the von Richthofen coat of arms—a pair of lions, signifying strength and fearlessness, placing a crown on the head of a judge. Richthofen displayed this family crest inside the castle too, in decorations of the rooms and on the family dishes and silver. High on another outside wall is the face of Barbarossa, the ancient King Frederick I of Germany, who, in legend, guarantees family happiness. His likeness is carved in three feet of sculptured red sandstone, and his resemblance to the baron is striking.

The castle inside was elegant with leaded glass in many of the windows and doors, and the walls were lined with leather inlaid with silver and gold. The estate itself was contained within an acre of walled grounds and originally consisted of twenty-one rooms. The new baroness was very impressed with the castle, but she balked at living out on the plains where there were no trees or

Gorgeous woodwork and leaded glass windows

flowers, so she bided her time in the luxury of the Albany Hotel as the baron constructed the Montclair ditch. It flowed from the High Line Canal at Windsor Lake and finally drained into the lowland where Montclair Park still stands. With available water now flowing through his "moat," the baron covered the castle grounds with trees from all over the world, and many flowers, particularly roses, a favorite of the baroness. Several blocks surrounding the castle were fenced to enclose deer and antelope. The baron was reported to even have a bear pit, and also two hundred canaries. Two dates are inscribed on the castle in stone: the first, 1887, is the year of the completion of the castle, which the baron called "Louiseburgh" in honor of his bride. The second date, 1888, is most probably the date Louise came to the castle.

Around the castle now sprouted his housing development—the new village of Montclair—with a "clear view of the mountains." For the next three years, the couple was in and out of the castle. The couple was able to travel the world as their housing parcels had sold well to the nouveau riche. Then came the recession of 1893, with the bottom falling out of the silver market, and as the fortunes of the miners collapsed with the economy, so went the housing market. Certainly the baron wasn't ruined,

Music room

but probably the heavy expense of living only part time in the castle seemed no longer feasible. The castle was put on the market and sold.

John N. Miller, a restaurateur who was also involved in the development of the area of Montclair, bought the castle and moved in with his family for the next eight years, while the Richthofens most probably moved back into a Denver hotel. Despite the change, the baron worked hard at developing "Montclair, The Beautiful Suburban Town of Denver, Colorado, U.S.A.,"

as his prospectus read. In 1898, he constructed the Molkerei or milkhouse, a sanitarium for tubercular patients, where patients were treated with fresh milk and sun baths. The dairy cattle were under the building and the patients above, as it was believed that inhaling the air from the barnyard would promote health, though there is no report on the success of this latter treatment. Later that same year, the baron contracted acute appendicitis and died of peritonitis at the age of forty-eight.

The Molkery

The Molkery (note spelling) still stands several hundred feet west of the castle, having survived near-demolition, and a stint as an asylum. In 1908, it was the first building in Denver to become a community center, and in 1909 underwent a total rejuvenation. Now capstone of a park for children, it is known as the Montclair Civic Building, and serves as headquarters for many local organizations such as the Montclair Women's Club. The city and county of Denver have given it landmark status.

Following the death of owner John Miller in 1902, the castle was purchased the next year by Edwin Hendrie who lived there with his family, renaming the structure Castlewood. It was Hendrie who, in 1910, added a west wing in the Tudor style, re-roofing the tower and parapets with tile, and adding a large paneled music room.

When the Hendrie daughter grew up, she married William W. Grant, and the couple took over the castle for the next twenty years. In 1924, Grant hired architect J.J.B. Benedict, who added a south wing and fourteen more rooms. This time, the owner went to great pains to match the original rhyolite stone, even opening the old quarry at Castle Rock to obtain a perfect match.

The castle was sold in 1937 to John Thams, Jr., with little or no changes, except for the name—now honoring its creator, Richthofen. In 1946, when Thams put the castle on the market, it was purchased by Fred G. Hunt, Jr., who had plans to convert it into a psychiatric hospital. However, the zoning request was denied, and later that same year the castle was sold to Etienne Pereyni and his wife, a Hungarian diplomat with an American wife, who with their own children

Finished in 1887, the castle stands starkly alone on the plains.

and many relatives, filled the castle for many years. Sally Cooper Murray who lived a block away has wonderful memories of playing with the Pereyni children and of the grand parties and concerts held there. It was also the Pereynis who sold off much of the land around the castle for eager homebuyers.

In 1971, Albert Purcell purchased the place, and stayed a single year before selling it to Dr. O. J. Seidens, who lived there with his family until around 1979. The Seidens were the family who experienced a variety of paranormal activity, explained later in the chapter. Lynn D. Anderson owned the castle in the early eighties but never occupied it. In 1980, the castle became a Designer Showcase for the Junior Symphony Guild, where each room was taken by a different designer. The public was charged a nominal fee to tour the rooms, and the profit went to support the Denver Symphony Orchestra. Two years later, vandals broke in, smashing windows and chandeliers, and causing $35,000 worth of damage, leaving a pretty big mess for the next buyer, the Priddy's, to clean up.

BARON WALTER VON RICHTHOFEN

Baron Walter von Richthofen was a member of an ancient and noble German family, born in Silesia, Germany, in 1848. The baron, caped, jovial, and bristling with bushy red whiskers was uncle and

godfather to the German flying ace, Manfred von Richthofen. Having fought himself in the Franco-Prussian and Austro-German wars, the baron had come to Denver in 1877, weary of the military life and ready to start anew. His first enterprise was the Downtown Denver Real Estate Company and he later helped found the Denver Chamber of Commerce. Very up and down in the business world, he achieved what seemed to be his first successful business venture by writing a book titled, *Cattle-Raising on the Plains of North America*. The profits allowed him to purchase a section on the plains that he planned to parcel off for elegant homes.

Divorcing his first wife, whom he sent to Germany to raise their two daughters, he became enamored with a peaches-and-cream divorcee,

Louise Ferguson Davies. He courted and won her over with lavish promises. He now began construction on his castle, first building the carriage house and living there as the castle grew. In 1888, the couple moved in. Not surprising for that era, the couple with divorces in their pasts, were shunned by Denver society, making it difficult for Louise, whose social contacts were now limited. Additionally, the baron was often off and running, promoting his Montclair and its "pure air and delightful climate" outside smoky and congested industrial Denver. He attracted buyers to his far-out suburb by furnishing free transportation from Denver using his "tallyhos" drawn by matched horses in glittering array, while along side rode the Baron in scarlet coat and breeches, accompanied by a pack of his great Russian wolfhounds.

The baron had lavish plans for his Montclair, including parks and tree-lined streets, a racetrack, gymnasium, swimming pool, theater, and art gallery. A connoisseur of art, he spent half a million dollars on a collection of European masters, charging the public twenty-five cents for admission. Unfortunately, the Denver public was offended by nude portraiture, and eventually the art gallery became the more acceptable casino. The crash of 1893 put an end to what then seemed a glorious future, with Richthofen struggling valiantly to save his multi-million dollar empire, and eventually ended up traveling Colorado with a wagon and team selling his books.

In 1898, the castle was sold and the Richthofens moved to Denver, while he continued to promote Montclair, and build the Molkerei. The

baron died of acute appendicitis, and his body was sent back to Germany where he is buried in the large Richthofen plot. Louise had a memorial fountain built to honor him, near the park close to the castle, and her ashes were interred there after her death in 1934.

SCANDAL

It must have been juicy gossip when a Baron, who sent his wife away to Europe and then divorced her, quickly married a woman who was not only a divorcee herself, but dyed her hair. Of course, the person to suffer was the woman—Louise. Although the neighbors would not visit, they allowed their children to come to the lavish parties the Richthofen's threw for children, especially at Christmas.

HAUNTED

In the 1970s, the owners were Dr. Seiden and his family, who reported several strange occurrences. Lights were seen in the tower one night with no

evidence of anyone having entered. When investigated, no footprints were found in the snow at the sole entrance, and the dust in the empty tower was undisturbed. Other experiences were hearing footsteps in empty passages and attics where there was no physical trace. The Priddys however, have experienced none of the strange phenomena, and perhaps the spirits have been laid to rest.

ACCESS

None. This castle is a private home, and the owners do not exhibit it.

DENVER AREA

South Broadway

Christian Church

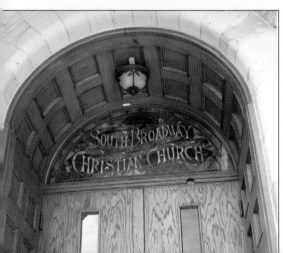

What's this all about? Here is a castle sitting on the corner of Ellsworth and Lincoln streets, and the name on it is South Broadway Christian Church, graven in stone no less. Weird, as it's neither on Broadway, nor is it in the section of Denver designated as south. Research revealed that it *was* originally on South Broadway, one block away, but just why it is built as a castle is still a mystery. Interestingly the architect, William Lang (see his biography in Castle Marne), duplicated this building in Colorado Springs, so it is he who must have been enamored by castles. So, a castle it is, with a tower, turret, stone edifice, and crenelation, and it has withstood many battles, financial in this case, in which the people gathered together and won. Proof of their victories is its spiffy, fresh look, its exterior wood trim a bright red against the gray rhyolite stone, and neat, colorful flower beds around its base.

Inside through the hall is a spacious meeting room with a great stained-glass window at its end. A kitchen adjoins the meeting room for servicing receptions and meetings. The church's basic structure is that of the traditional cross, evident in the sanctuary although invisible from the street. Here, Gothic arches predominate throughout, with intricate, interlaced, groined vaults on the north and south sides of the ceiling. In between the wood moldings in the ceiling is a fleur-de-lis pattern pressed into rolled sheets of tin and painted

Stucco molding surrounds the sanctuary

pale cream. The windows are Gothic as well. Additional original décor is the wide stucco molding atop the wainscoting and also embellishing the baptismal font. About a foot in height, the molding—a raised plaster strip of flower medallions pointed white and tipped with gold—surrounds the sanctuary.

The gigantic pipes of the organ are the most prominent feature in the sanctuary, originally

Baptismal font

installed in 1907, and nestled behind the altar on a raised stage. A new purchase is a Rogers digital console, previously featured at the Aspen Music Festival. More grant money from Historic Denver will allow the old and the new to be interfaced in the next year or so, making the church's sound system one of the best in the city.

To the right of the stage is the baptismal font that you could almost swim laps in. Light filters in through massive stained-glass windows on the left, which have been dedicated to and provided by the founders of the church. In fact, three of the four walls have large stained-glass windows, but the windows to the north receive no sunlight as they are attached to the addition added in the 1950s. Future plans are to replace this addition with one more suitable to the church's architecture.

Pastor Mark Pumphrey leads the worship services on Sunday, and is given credit for increasing the congregation up to its present 250 members. But much more goes on than just church services. There are five community-minded merchants in the vicinity who provide food for their Sandwich Ministry, which meets every Tuesday night. On Wednesday morning, they deliver 275 lunches to the Eleventh Avenue Hotel to provide brown bag lunches for men seeking work.

The church is host to many outside groups that meet here. These include organizations like the Denver Classical Guitar Society as well as recovery groups like the several 12-Step self-help programs. Some rooms are used by Denver Free University for their language classes. A series of classical concerts is also planned from September through May. Information on any of these activities is available on their website at www.southbroadwaychristian church.org or by calling 303-722-4679.

Balconies in reception room

HISTORY OF THE CASTLE

In 1888 John Sutton, an engineer and a religious man, lost his wife, Henrietta, when a fall in the garden severely injured her, causing her death. The next year, Sutton enlisted the help of the Reverend Bayard Craig, who had given them solace in Henrietta's final hours. Sutton wanted to memorialize her by building a church, and to verify his dedication, Sutton offered $12,000, a large sum at that time, as a down payment on a new building. The two men, together with thirty-six other people, met in January of 1890, and created South Broadway Christian Church, first meeting at a large tent located between Ellsworth and Bayaud on Broadway, on the grounds where Sutton lived. In the next two-and-a-half years, the congregation grew to some six hundred people while the permanent building was being planned and built. Colorado Governor John Routt, a member, laid the cornerstone for the church in 1891, with Henrietta Sutton's Bible placed under it. One year later, the church was officially dedicated. Eight hundred children, gathered from the Christian churches throughout Denver, marched from the tent to the new building for the opening.

John Sutton's twelve thousand dollars had given a leg up for the building but there was still a great deal of debt. Selling his house, Sutton donated an additional $30,000, asking that in return he be allowed to live in two rooms of the tower. His wish, of course, was granted, and for the next nine years, until the end of his life, "Uncle" John, as he was known, lived in his two-room apartment in the tower.

An interesting sidelight is that the first music director for the church was Professor Wilberforce Whiteman, father of orchestra leader Paul Whiteman, who directed the music of the church while baby Paul slept in the front pew during the services.

A remarkable thing about this church, actually about its congregation, has been the response it gives to financial problems. One year after the church opened its doors, the economic depression of 1893 hit Denver hard, making the church's debt a threatening issue. Prior to the depression, their real estate holdings had well covered their payments, but with the great devaluation of their properties, the church was quite suddenly in debt. Notified, the congregation pulled together enough money to meet its obligations, and by 1905, the mortgage was paid off. In several situations since, the members have rallied to take care of emergencies, often financial. The church currently also owns several lots to the north as well as the lot directly east, and will reconfigure when the new addition is built.

The designation as an Historical Landmark in 1969 by Historic Denver has helped the church receive grants for restoration. In 2005, the grant helped to seal the foundation, and in 2006, the exterior was cleaned and painted. The 2007 funds will put great music back into a great church.

JOHN SUTTON

Without the dedication of this man, this church would never have existed. Coming to Colorado with his wife, Henrietta, in 1896, John Sutton lived at 80 South Broadway in a home on a large lot. With the death of his wife, he became more and more committed to a church dedicated to her memory, and it was here on his property on Broadway that a large tent, or tabernacle, was put up to house the first congregation.

When he retired from selling real estate, he had many holdings in Denver, and seems to have given them all to the church for income. Selling his home and donating the proceeds of $30,000 correlates with the year of the silver devaluation, and was probably most vital in keeping the church from going under.

John Sutton became very ill at the end of his life, but insisted on staying in the church. While possible, the congregation nursed him in a room in the basement, until the demands of his care became prohibitive, and against his wishes, he was moved to a friend's house where he died in February of 1901. He is buried in Denver in the Riverside Cemetery.

Stairs to the tower

HAUNTED

Many haunted house stories have very logical explanations for the strange noises, footsteps, or eerie happenings, but the goings-on here are pretty hard to contribute to natural causes.

Somebody lives in the church, and some guess it's Uncle John. "He" is a talented fellow, and plays the organ when the church is dark and the organ is shut up. Once a member, Dustin Adkins, was vacuuming, with the cord coiled at his feet, when the vacuum stopped. Dustin turned to find the plug on the floor. Puzzled, he plugged it back in and again started vacuuming, when it quit again. This time, the plug was on the floor and four feet from the outlet, and it was obvious that tension had not caused the cord to pull out. Dustin left—in a big hurry.

Rochelle Chartier, president of the Denver Classical Guitar Society, was at the church alone late one evening. Pushing on the front door, she just couldn't get it to open, though she tried for several minutes. Finally, and quite suddenly, the door released and opened with the greatest of ease. She left again for more boxes and the problem repeated itself. Never before or since has the door stuck, and never again has Rochelle stayed late alone.

There's nothing mean about the entity, and he confines himself to the original, or old, part of the church, never crossing the doorway into the new building. He does have a mischievous nature however. Personnel hear boards creaking as he walks across the floor above where they are working. This happens both when they're in the basement or on the first floor, and when the church is otherwise empty.

There's just no visible person around, though he can be felt, especially in the basement. Chris Vitt, the secretary, has been there for years, and just accepts him, since many incidents happen when the church is locked and there's no possibility of another person being there. "He plays the piano too," she added. "I heard a single note tune being played, but it stopped when I opened the door. No one was there, of course."

An interesting sidenote—Baron von Richthofen built a beer garden, his Sans Souci, on "the corner of Ellsworth and Lincoln," and quite probably on this very spot. Another possibility—maybe it's just someone after a beer.

ACCESS
Absolutely, and you're welcome almost any time. Closed on Mondays however. For information on group meetings, call secretary Chris Vitt at 303-722-4679.

Springer Castle

(Highlands Ranch Mansion)

At one time, it could be seen from a hundred miles away—a castle atop a rise overlooking 22,000 acres of cattle ranch. Now it's sequestered like the Queen Bee, hidden in a labyrinth of twisted streets lined with modern houses. The original Springer Castle, currently the property of Shea Homes, is still a working cattle ranch. Besides the castle itself, the castle complex has a bunk house for ranch hands, an equipment barn for horse-shoeing and storage, three extra barns for calving and branding, and a great stone windmill seen silhouetted against the horizon, far up on a hill to the south. This is what remains of the original homestead, which is tucked into the remaining 250 acres located inside the incorporated city of Highlands Ranch. The cattle, some 650 to 1000 head, are raised in southern Highlands Ranch, now called the Backcountry Wilderness Area.

The approach to the castle is through two iron gates; the first warning private access and the second, enclosing a barrier of trees, which in turn surrounds the manicured grounds and the castle. The castle itself is constructed of hand-hewn granite, wood, brick, and stucco. The crenelated square tower housing the entrance stands at the east end of a long porch with a backdrop of a vine-covered wall. Through the heavy wood doors is a spacious entry with a staircase straight ahead to the second floor, and a wide arch at the right into the great hall.

Top: "Skating" room; below: Built-in clock near the entry of the guest hall.

Although a castle outside, the interior is proof that the many families owning it and living here maintained it as a ranch. Located in the center of the wall of the great hall is a carved stone fireplace, which at one time opened into two rooms, but now serves only this one. Its stonework is etched with symbols from the Kistler era, with the brand of Diamond K repeated across the top, and etchings of the castle and outbuildings beneath the brands. To the left, built into the wall near the entry, is a large clock. It was imported from Germany and is of ornately carved ebony Italian woodwork, and weighs two tons. This room, originally the ballroom, is used now as it was in John Springer's day, when the castle was newly built.

Immediately behind the great hall is the billiard room with its butterfly inlays used to anchor the oak paneling together. The entire room has no

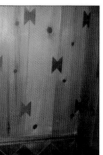

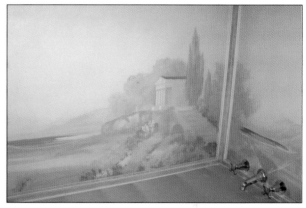

nails but relies on the tight-fitting ceiling molding and inlays for support. To the right and behind the great hall is a much larger room, flooded with light. The long south wall is lined with windows overlooking the back garden, and the walls are papered to look very much like marble. The floor is an inlaid terrazzo, some forty feet across, and legend has it that the children of Lawrence Phipps, Jr. used this room for roller skating. This room opens onto a long wrap-around covered porch that extends around the corner facing west and across the north frontage clear to the entrance.

A curved stairway from the entry leads to the upper floor and seven bedrooms, with a seven foot wide hallway in between. These bedrooms share five baths, where the most interesting features are the hand-painted figures. Graceful birds are in one area, while the "Asian" bath is done in red with Oriental themes of golden bamboo stalks and long-tailed birds.

Hand-painted bathrooms

Straight through the entry is the kitchen, still vintage 1920s. The servants' quarters, accessible only from the second floor, are above the kitchen and extend outward over an arched courtyard entry below. This small courtyard is bordered on the east side by a building of river-rock stone, originally built to hold a one-lane bowling alley, while a large, six-car garage sits at the south end. The barns are beyond. The backyard faces due south and gives a superb view of the surrounding area. Particularly striking is the stone windmill, silhouetted against the sky on a distant hill.

The date "1891" in stone on exterior.

Altogether, the castle is 22,000 square feet, with a total of fourteen bedrooms, eleven bathrooms, five fireplaces, the great room, a ballroom, dining room, billiard room, library, and kitchen.

The Shea Company is now the owner and guardian of the property, maintaining it and honoring it as an historical treasure. It is frequently used by the Highlands Ranch Community Association and the Highlands Ranch Historical Society for special occasions and by special permission. (See "Guide to Availability" at the end of the book.)

HISTORY OF THE CASTLE

The castle itself is mysterious, as the builder is unknown. The date in stone near the entrance is 1891, which would indicate the date of completion. However, because the land was purchased for cash and not homesteaded, it was not subject to government scrutiny, and the builder is therefore unrecorded.

John Springer and his ailing wife, Eliza, first came to Colorado in 1896, and two years later, bought the castle along with 5,000 acres. Several years later, he expanded his acreage to a total of 12,000 by buying up the small farms around him.

John Springer was a lawyer, banker, and cattleman, but his first love was horses, and it was he who set up the ranch soon renowned as the John Springer Cross Country Horse and Cattle Ranch. Eliza, fragile in health and suffering from tuberculosis, died in 1904 before she was forty years old. Five years later, Springer met his second wife, Isabelle, a newly divorced but apparently stun-

ning creature. Springer, quite smitten, renamed his home the Castle Isabelle.

A mere two years later, Isabelle was in the middle of a scandalous murder, of which she had been the catalyst. Springer filed for divorce five days after the murder, and in 1913 sold the ranch to the father of his first wife, Colonel William Hughes, a cattle baron himself, who also owned the largest cattle ranch in Texas. Hughes renamed the Springer property Sunland Ranch, and when he died in 1918, left the estate to his granddaughter Annie—John and Eliza Springer's daughter.

A daughter of a foreman who had lived on the ranch as a child around that time, recalls the interior had rustic western décor. The floors were

Fireplace located in the great hall.

covered with Navajo rugs and the drapes made of dyed doeskin. Furniture was made from deer antlers, or was massive and ornately carved. An elaborate punch bowl stand, also of deer antlers, held seventy-two cups, which hung from the prongs.

In 1920 Annie and her husband Lafayette Hughes (coincidental last names) sold the Sunland Ranch to Waite Phillips, whose brothers had founded Phillips Oil Company. (It was during this period of prohibition that the ranch was reputed to harbor a still or two where squatters mashed out their whiskey.) A mere six years later it was bought by Frank E. Kistler and established as the Diamond K Ranch, where Kistler raised Angus cattle, purebred sheep, chickens, and hogs.

Kistler hired architect J.B.B. Benedict (see Summer White House) to plan extensive renovations to the mansion. They added a west wing styled in English Tudor, featuring a shake-shingle

Windmill

roof, gables, and carved wood trim. Fireplaces were added, the largest in the great room with the Diamond K brand etched across the top and scenes of the castle and grounds below. Hardwood floors were put in and two secret panels inserted into the wood between the great hall and the billiard room. Benedict's elaborate plan included a one-lane bowling alley built directly east of the castle in its own stone building. But as ideal as the Kistler's life seemed, their marriage hit the rocks in 1929. After a quick divorce, Kistler immediately married Leana Antonides, widow of a Denver oilman. When his first wife, Florence, moved out, she took three of the four children with her; the youngest, Julia, chose to stay with her father. Tragically for the child, her father poured out his affection on his new wife's two sons, leaving Julia emotionally abandoned.

Kistler had many friends in the elite Arapahoe Hunt Club—hunters on horseback with hounds in the old English tradition. The A. H. C. had originally used the grounds of the Denver Country Club to ride to the chase, but were now invited to the vast, open hills of the Diamond K Ranch. Hunt Master of this group was Lawrence C. Phipps, Jr., and in 1937, when Kistler was in financial difficulty, Phipps purchased the castle and grounds from him, renaming it Highland Ranch. Six years later, in 1943, Phipps added 3,380 acres to the ranch by purchasing the adjoining Welte Dairy Farm, which had been a neighbor for sixty-six years. Added to his other holdings, this brought the total acreage of the ranch to its present 23,000.

Springer added the crenelated tower

The castle seemed to be hard on marriages. One year after purchase, the Phipps were divorced—she moving out with the children. In 1945, Phipps married again. His second wife, Elaine, was an artist, and it is her talented work seen in the bathrooms today.

The ranch stayed with the Phipps family until his death in 1976. Lawrence Phipps III was executor of the estate and he put the ranch on the market. It was purchased by Marvin Davis, owner of Davis Oil Corporation, who organized the Highlands Ventures Corporation, and two years later the entire operation was bought by the

Mission Viejo Company for housing development. Construction began in 1980. One year later, being the first home owners, Phil and Kaye Scott were presented with a gift of a 650-pound steer. In 1997 Shea Homes purchased the whole kit and caboodle, and are now the sole owners of what has become the incorporated city of Highlands Ranch, which includes the castle and grounds as well.

JOHN W. SPRINGER

John W. Springer was born in 1859 in Jacksonville, Illinois, the son of a prominent attorney. His uncle was a member of Congress, and after law school, sent Springer to clerk in Washington, D.C., where he became interested in politics and the workings of the government. After moving to Texas, he married Eliza Clifton Hughes in Dallas in 1891. She bore him a daughter, Annie, but it soon became evident that Eliza was becoming very ill with the dreaded disease, tuberculosis. Treatment then was a high, dry climate, which drew many victims to the high plains of Colorado.

Coming to Denver in 1896, Springer was a practicing lawyer with banking investments and political ambitions, but his true love was horses. He bought the castle in 1898 and many of the smaller holdings around it, consolidating them into the largest landholding in the region, and raising prize-winning stock of both cattle and horses. He also began additional construction on the castle, adding an extra crenelated tower and transforming the original building into his royal residence.

Springer's coach-and-fours were well known around the streets of Denver until the automobile made coaches passé. Ironically, he also worked for the improvement of the dirt roads, and pushed to create the original paved road connecting Denver to Littleton—Colorado's first modern highway.

As businessman, Springer had founded the Continental Trust and was director of the Capital Bank. Raising cattle, he questioned the practice of shipping cattle East to be slaughtered when they were raised in the West, so he formed the National Livestock Association, of which the local packing industry became an outgrowth, after overcoming severe opposition from eastern competitors.

His most famous political moments happened in 1904. Springer, a staunch Republican, not only ran for mayor of Denver but also was endorsed as a nominee for national vice president under Teddy Roosevelt by the Colorado Republicans. Unfortunately, neither worked out, and he lost his wife that year as well.

Five years later, Springer met and married his second wife, Isabelle Paterson, a very beautiful, and newly divorced, young woman. Unfortunately, Isabelle, his charming "Sassy," had several bad habits—among them narcotics, nightlife, and a taste for adventure. For this charmer, one man was not enough, and in 1911, one of her lovers murdered another in the Brown Palace bar. Adding insult to injury, her husband had rented a suite in the luxurious Brown so that his wife, shopping in the city, would have a place to stay. It was

Great room

there, in the sixth floor suite of the Brown Palace, that Isabelle Springer threw parties that were the talk of the town.

Springer, who had a reputation as an upstanding and honest citizen, was appalled by the scandal. He immediately filed for a divorce and sold the property to his first father-in-law, William Hughes, so the Castle Isabelle was no more.

It is quite possible that Springer never did live in the castle himself. He is listed as selling his home at Eighteenth and Williams streets in Denver in 1900, and later owning a home at 930 Washington when married to Isabelle. Running

for mayor of Denver would require his living in the city itself, and also, he was a member of the Denver Chamber of Commerce. I would hazard a guess that, following the sale of his ranch, he simply settled into a law practice in the city.

In 1936, Springer met and married a Scottish woman, Janethe Lovate, and his last home was in Littleton at 250 Windemere Street. Springer died in 1945 and is buried in the Littleton Cemetery.

SCANDAL

Springer was a man of impeccable family and background. His family was of German descent and traceable back to 1089. Reputation was what he strove for his entire life, and the scandal with Isabelle must have just about unhinged him. For a complete scenario on this escapade, read Dick Kreck's book, *Murder at the Brown Palace*. It's a good one.

As a postscript, Isabelle died in April of 1917 in the Pauper's Hospital, Blackwell's Island, N.Y. This was a mere six years following her divorce, her beauty now ravaged by alcohol and drugs.

HAUNTED

We have a yes on this one. Most prominent is the ghost of Julia Kistler, daughter of the fifth owner, whose father emotionally abandoned her for his

stepsons. There are claims that her figure has been seen silhouetted in her bedroom window on days the castle was known to be vacant, and her soft, anguished sobs have been heard by several workers throughout the upper halls.

Other odd incidences have occurred in the castle. Several years back, the mammoth clock in the great hall was heard to chime during a meeting, although the mechanism has been out of order for years.

Caroline Smith, docent and president of the Highlands Ranch Historical Society, reports a day when, waiting for a group of school children, she suddenly smelled a strong bouquet of flowers, although there were none in the building. Later, a mother commented on the aroma as well.

ACCESS

The castle is owned and run by the Shea Company. Events are allowed there only for special groups like the Highlands Ranch Community Association, the Metro District of Highlands Ranch, and the Highlands Ranch Historical Society. For information on these events, call Jamie Noebel at 303-791-2500, or Caroline Smith at 303-471-5611.

DIRECTIONS: Broadway to Highlands Ranch Blvd. Turn east and go to Ranch Road. Turn left. Public access not available.

COLORADO SPRINGS AREA

Glen Eyrie Castle

The setting here is spectacular—so fairy-tale magnificent that the castle seems almost secondary. The Glen Eyrie Complex is sequestered on an area of more that 880 lush acres, and includes the castle, carriage house, and several other living quarters. All are in a small valley surrounded by gargantuan pilasters and tilted slabs of dark red sandstone, harbingers of the nearby Garden of the Gods.

Founder of the city of Colorado Springs and builder of the castle, General William J. Palmer first built his home and outbuildings here in 1870 and draped them with acres of lawn that he studded with trees of many native and exotic varieties, today soaring to tremendous heights. It's in this wooded glen (glen of the eagle's aerie) and idyllic setting that the stone castle, complete with tower and Gothic windows, sits like a page out of a child's picture book.

In Tudor style, the castle has sixty-seven rooms, with extensive quarter-sawn oak paneling on the main floor cut to best expose the grain of the wood. Central is a chimney serving four fireplaces, each in a separate room. Most charming is the tea room decorated in Wedgwood blue with white trim. Public and private teas are held here daily, again giving the castle a feel of the past. The main floor holds all the common areas that include the dining room, lounge, and of course, the reception room. The warmth of the surrounding

Castle cuddled against the Garden of the Gods.

Top: Wedgewood blue tea room. Bottom: Elegant dining

wood paneling and the smaller-sized rooms maintain the feeling of intimacy lacking in a commercial hotel. A man of foresight, Palmer added a central vacuum system, electricity, and extensive plumbing, as well as carefully designed chimneys to keep the smoke from polluting the area. To Palmer and his staff's great credit, many systems still function today with very little repair needed.

Rooms on the upper floors are replicated in Victorian style, with furnishings and wallpaper closely copied from the many photographs taken when Palmer lived there. The fourth level is now a special suite often used by honeymooners or visiting dignitaries.

A passageway on the second floor leads to a large ballroom, which is really this castle's great hall, complete with a loft for orchestra or audience. Here every Christmas a Renaissance Ball is held,

complete with costumed entertainment and serving persons. Titled the Madrigal Banquet, anyone wishing to attend may buy tickets, but it is recommended that reservations be made by September or at latest, mid-October, due to its popularity.

Today the castle is owned and run by the ministry and international headquarters of The Navigators, a fundamental Christian group. Although the building itself is often used for retreats, Christian fellowship, and missionary training, the castle's many sumptuous period bedrooms are available to the public, with breakfast included in the King James dining room.

HISTORY OF THE CASTLE

Pikes Peak played a very vital role in the development of this entire area. General William J. Palmer, Civil War veteran and hero, first viewed the mountain in 1869 while scouting for a railroad route through the Rocky Mountains for the Kansas Pacific Railroad, part of the Union Pacific. Fascinated with the area, he purchased 10,000 acres of land at $1.25 per acre to establish the Fountain Colony, the town later to become Colorado Springs. Additionally, he chose 2,225 prime acres in a lush valley near the Garden of the Gods where he promised to build for his bride, Queen, "the grandest of homes." They married in 1870, and honeymooned in Europe for four months while their new home was under construction.

The general and his "Queen" first lived in the carriage house while their home, a twenty-two room house of adobe and wood, was being built. Completed in 1872, they moved in and later remodeled, adding a tower and additional rooms, as a "castle" was part of their dreams for the future. By 1882 electricity was added, and a plumber had completed a system of waterworks to include three fountains. By this time, Mrs. Palmer and the general had three daughters.

But there seemed to be trouble brewing, as rail wars were going on between railroad companies, and Palmer had a fear of his young daughters being kidnapped. He built a school for them on the castle grounds and imported a German schoolmistress. Then in 1880, Queen suffered a small heart attack and was advised by her doctor to move to a lower elevation. She and the children spent the rest of her life first on the East Coast and later in England. Queen never returned to Glen Eyrie as she died in 1894 at the age of forty-four.

The school house

Top: Carefully crafted stonework; above: fireplace in great room

In this same period, Fountain Colony had grown to 1500 residents, bringing prosperity to the Palmers. Palmer was keeping a promise to his deceased wife when he remodeled his adobe and wood home into a castle in 1904. Leaving only the chimney from the original structure, the castle was built with age-old weathered stones from the Bear Creek area, and carefully crafted by the stone cutters to fit together almost without masonry. And it must have been a trying job for the masons, as chisels and mallets were not allowed to disturb the natural growth of lichen on the stones. As the

home was uninhabitable during construction, Palmer and his three daughters toured Europe for two years, collecting fireplaces, artifacts, and antiques, some from cathedrals and castles that he felt would authenticate his castle. He had electricity in his house since 1882, as well as extensive plumbing. Additionally, the castle had telephones and a central vacuum system, as well as pollution control on the smoke from the twenty-four fireplaces. This was indeed the home of the future.

The castle was completed and ready for occupancy in 1905. Originally, the second floor held

Top: The great hall.
*Bottom left and right: Victorian-style bedrooms are
replications from photographs.*

bedrooms for the family, while the third floor was
designed as rooms for guests and visitors. It
appears that the fourth floor was an artists' studio.

Palmer was to enjoy his new home for merely
a year before suffering a fall that put him in a
wheelchair for the remaining three years of his
life. However, during the Christmas seasons, the
local children were always invited to the castle

great hall and given presents, all selected personally by Palmer. He also continued to entertain friends and give to the community.

He died at the age of 72, with the estate valued at over three million dollars. His daughters put the estate on the market, where it was finally purchased in 1916 by a group of Oklahoma businessmen. They platted the grounds for residential development and planned a country club setting with the castle as club house and the grounds a golf course. Their timing was poor, however, as the country was in the middle of World War I and no one seemed interested in country club living.

One entrepreneur after another purchased the property until 1953, when a real estate broker in Colorado Springs contacted Billy Graham, who was looking for a headquarters for his ministry. Although Reverend Graham did not buy it, he referred it to Dawson Trotman, founder of The Navigators, a Christian group that was very interested. With no money for a down payment, they appealed to the public, and raised $110,000 in six weeks. Currently the castle, with its grounds intact and an additional 300 acres adjoining the mountain reservoir at the head of Queen's Canyon, belong to The Navigators and is their world headquarters, where they sponsor and focus on Christian "Life Changing" Retreats.

GENERAL WILLIAM J. PALMER

As an historic figure, General William J. Palmer was very vital in the development of Colorado. He was founder of Colorado Springs and the Denver and Rio Grande Railway, and gifted the state many philanthropic institutions that include Colorado College, Colorado School for the Deaf and Blind, a tuberculosis sanitarium, and altogether, some three million dollars for development.

Born in Delaware, William Jackson Palmer's Quaker family soon moved to Pennsylvania where he was raised. His fascination with rail travel began at a very young age as he watched the steam locomotives come by near his home. He was only in his late teens and working for the engineering corps of Hemfield Railroad, when he was selected by officials to be sent to Europe to study the systems that had been developed in England and France. His career was interrupted by the onset of the Civil War in 1861, when, though complicated by his Quaker background, he was compelled to enlist because of his compassion for slaves. Palmer enlisted and raised up an elite troop of cavalry for the Union forces, later leading many successful campaigns, until by age

73

The grounds of Glen Eyrie support abundant wildlife

The original carriage house overshadowed by the Gardens of the Gods.

Choosing the best area of the best, Palmer bought an additional 2,225 acres for his own use, and here he brought his bride, Queen, when he married in 1870. That same year, Palmer created the Denver and Rio Grande Railway with the intent of running the line clear into Mexico. This was the first narrow gauge rail to run in the area, which Palmer used to adapt to the twisted mountain passageways.

Palmer lived in his wood and adobe home until 1904 when he demolished the original structure and built his stone castle in memory of his wife.

An avid horseman, Palmer kept a stable of horses, riding almost daily over the grounds at Glen Eyrie. In 1906, while out on the trail, his horse stumbled, tossing him to the ground. His neck was broken by the fall, paralyzing him from the third rib down. Down but not out, Palmer continued to entertain friends from a wheel chair for the three remaining years of his life.

twenty-nine, he had become the second youngest brigadier general, second only to General Custer. Even though he was highly decorated, he chose military discharge after the war to follow his passion of railroading.

On a scouting trip for the eastern division of the Union Pacific Railroad he discovered the Pikes Peak area. With his own money he bought land to develop a community that was modern and civilized. On 10,000 acres of land he opened up Fountain Colony where neither saloons nor gambling houses were allowed. Even the sale of alcohol was illegal, and remained that way until 1933 when prohibition was rescinded.

SCANDAL

None, certainly, with the general. Yet it is a bit ironic that his carriage house was turned into a tavern by the purchasers of the estate in 1916. Named The Black Horse Tavern, probably after Palmer's horse, "Señor," it allowed alcohol onto the very grounds originally owned by Palmer, who was dead-set against drinking.

HAUNTED

No spirits found yet.

ACCESS

Although basically a Christian conference center, Glen Eyrie is accessible to the public, and rooms in the castle can be rented at rates of from $50 to $190 per night. Teas and tours of the castle and grounds are available on weekdays at a minimal charge. By reservation only. Call 1-800-944-4536. For further information, see their website at www.gleneyrie.org.

DIRECTIONS: I-25 to exit 146. Go west on Garden of the Gods Road 2+ miles to a "T," which is 30th Street. Left for .6 miles. It will be on your right with the word "Navigator" on a stone block. Turn right, then left to the Glen Eyrie Conference Center. Address: 3820 N. 30th Street, Colorado Springs.

COLORADO SPRINGS AREA

Miramont Castle

THE CASTLE TODAY

A multitude of mysteries surround this strange castle. Why did its owner vanish five years after pouring his family fortune and goods into a life-long dream? Where are the missing staircases known to have existed, and why the secret passage behind the north wall? It now appears there are two rooms as yet undiscovered, small alcoves tucked in against the mountain. New facts are uncovered almost daily and often in unusual ways.

The castle itself is stair-stepped up the mountainside and firmly anchored to bedrock, with the front door on the first level and the back door on the fourth. Miramont has forty-six rooms, one an octagon, another with sixteen walls, two conservatory greenhouses, grand staircases, lost staircases, secret passages, and rarely a room with four square corners. The creator of the castle was Father Jean Baptiste Francolon, a priest originally from France, who lived in the castle with his widowed mother, Marie. Although only a few minor pieces of the Francolon furnishings survive, the newspaper descriptions give evidence—a mahogany table inlaid with jewels, for example—that the Francolon family was aristocratic and wealthy, and that the palace was furnished with tapestries, oils, statuary, antique vestments, and laces, as well as an art collection for which a gallery was built. The gallery is now a museum of the Victorian age and set up as if awaiting dinner guests for a gala event.

Windows are architecturally diverse

Top: Drawing room. Bottom: Drawing room stone fireplace

As you enter the front door on the bottom level, you are in what was the basement level in the original castle. It now holds the entry room and the Museum of Miniatures, with its display of international buildings and dolls, and a fascinating section replicating early Manitou and Colorado Springs. The staircase on the right leads up to the drawing room and provides the best representation of the castle's past glory. Midway up is a stained-glass window donated by, and dedicated to, Lillian and Ivan Gragg, a family who mortgaged their home to save the castle from demolition. They represent a community with a

Top: Guest bedroom with sixteen sides.
Right: Dining room—note copper ceiling.

pioneer work-together spirit reported more fully in the section on the castle history.

On the second level, the gargantuan fireplace in the drawing room itself weighs over 400,000 pounds and is seated on bedrock. Above the fireplace are African mahogany shingles, which are original as is the Victorian red of the walls. The ceiling is painted with thinly rolled sheets of gold leaf, powdered, and made into a paint, the cost of which would be prohibitive in today's market. A rounded, Oriental-style arch leads into the piano room, while a Byzantine arch leads into the drawing room itself. The wallpapers in the hallway, dining room, and kitchen are documented, meaning they are copies of wallpaper that existed there in 1896. In fact, the only original wallpaper in the

Top: Priest's bedroom; middle: Marie's bedroom; bottom: chapel library

house is at the back of a small bathroom in a closet under the stairs. And practically speaking, this is a very good thing since many wallpapers in the Victorian era had been dyed with an arsenic compound that was very poisonous. On the positive side, there are no bugs in that closet.

Beyond the drawing room, a double glass door leads to a terrace area, now the Queen's Parlor Tea Room. This was originally a greenhouse covered by a greenhouse glass shell. Also on this level is a stained-glass window given in memory of Guy Boyd, another major mover whom the castle may thank for its present existence.

Additionally, the second level holds the music room, a formal dining room, a library, and a kitchen with the components of that era. The square piano was constructed prior to 1875, and is veneered with rosewood and has ivory keys. What is now the chapel was most probably the priest's library, an eight-sided room with a floor of chevron-patterned hardwood. Adjoining the chapel is the guest bedroom with its sixteen sides, which must have been a challenge for placing furniture. It has a dressing room and bath, as well as a solid brass fireplace.

All furnishings, though not of the Francolons, are of a vintage age, donated by families of the area and significant to local history. The dining room oak table and chairs are over one hundred years old, and the china is as well. Egg cartons in the cupboards are of the same era, but the stemware is dated from around 1800.

On the third level are the three rooms of Marie Francolon's suite, consisting of her bed-

Keyhole windows

room, bath, and dressing room. Marie's own bed had once belonged to the Empress Josephine, and was shipped to America in pieces and reassembled in this room. The four posters were some fourteen feet tall, and had to be cut down to fit in the room. In 1945, the bed was removed from the castle and disappeared. We know what it looked like because of the photo displayed in this room. Original costumes and vintage photos of the area authenticate a feeling of the 1890s.

Outside Marie's bedroom is the great hall, now used for dining but was originally the art gallery displaying the priest's extensive art collec-

tion, including a painting by Velázquez and a wood carving of Benevenuto Cellini. The priest's quarters are in the front of the castle facing south and of minimal interest.

A small staircase leads to the fourth floor, now a charming Victorian gift shop with historic displays in three of the rooms formerly belonging to the servants. Tucked under the eaves, these folks were either quite short or had to stoop a lot, but the view is magnificent. This is also the exit level where you can proceed down the stairs to the gardens and to the building that was once the miniature railroad museum, but in the future will be a gift shop.

Miramont before east wing added, circa 1896. Original home, Montcalme, far left.

HISTORY OF THE CASTLE

Indecision or nostalgia? It's hard to decide which frame of mind belonged to Father Jean Baptiste Francolon when he planned Miramont Castle in 1895. A native of France and the son of a world-roving diplomat, he incorporated nine separate styles of architecture at random throughout his Manitou Springs leviathan—styles he'd no doubt seen and admired as a child and adolescent. The castle accoutrements therefore range from the medieval, castellated, crenelated battlements, to the shingle-style Queen Anne roof and the Gothic front door. The result is certainly "interesting" to use real estate-ese for bizarre.

An ailing Father Francolon had arrived in Manitou Springs to partake of the mineral waters in the summer of 1892, and his widowed mother, Marie, followed him a year later. In 1895 the priest began a collaboration with contractor Angus Gillis, a Scott who later built many major buildings in the Pikes Peak area and became quite famous and an important contributor to the area in his own right. Interestingly, Angus Gillis was the builder of El Paso County's first electrical generator, and the castle featured both running water and electricity when it was built. Most probably, the priest moved into the castle he called Miramont in 1896, with the east wing finished a year later when his mother moved in. Father Francolon then deeded their original frame home, which sat on the clearing right above the castle, to the Sisters of Mercy to use as a sanitarium for patients with health problems, who had come to Manitou seeking the healing waters. It was a trade-off. The Sisters then contracted to care for the Father in his old age. And yet….

Father Francolon and his mother occupied the castle for only a brief period of less than five years. Then quite abruptly, they left.

The castle was vacant from 1900 to 1904, when the Sisters of Mercy used it in conjunction with a German doctor named Kneipp, who administered a "water cure" involving the healing mineral waters nearby. In 1904, a fire in the furnace room of the original Francolon home, just above and to the west of the castle, destroyed the wooden structure, which was housing the patients. The Sisters then purchased the castle itself to become their new hospital. The Sisters made a number of changes to the building, adapting it to the needs of their patients and the patients' families, some of whom also lived there. They also renamed their institution Montcalme as this had been the designation for their facility in the neighboring frame home.

Montcalme remained a sanitarium until 1928 when the Sisters could no longer economically afford to treat patients. It then became a retreat for the Order with other rooms rented to tourists until it was sold in 1946. The new owners created an apartment complex of ten large apartments and restored the name to Miramont. With the creation of the Manitou Springs Historical Society and a grant from the Centennial-Bicentennial Commission, the castle was purchased in 1976 for the purpose of restoring it to its original Victorian state. And herein lies a tale of true heroism.

In a dismal state of repair, the castle had been condemned by the city of Manitou and was scheduled to be demolished in 1976. The people of Manitou, under the leadership of the Lillian and Ivan Graggs, gathered together. Determined that their historical castle would not be torn down, they and twenty-five other families mortgaged their own homes in order to buy the property. The community unified, with everyone pitching in for the reconstruction. The Boy Scouts, the Girl Scouts, the school children, and the newly formed Manitou Historical Society as organizer, scraped, hauled, painted, donated, and refurbished the castle into its original state. Thus, it was only by the heroic actions of the Manitou Historical Society and the many, many volunteers involved that the castle regained its past beauty. In 1977, Miramont Castle was added to the National Register of Historical Places, achieving national landmark status.

FATHER JEAN BAPTISTE FRANCOLON

Born in France in 1854, Jean Baptiste Francolon was the son of a wealthy diplomat in a strongly Catholic family. He came to the United States in 1878 as a priest, and was first secretary to Archbishop Lamy in Santa Fe, later given charge of the development of many mission churches among the Native Americans in the area. In the early 1890s Father Francolon fell ill from a stomach complaint and transferred to the Manitou area because of the healing waters there. Here he built his original home, a frame structure above the castle's present loca-

Marie Francolon

tion. He immediately began planning for the castle to be built with contractor Angus Gillis, using unique architectural combinations of many sorts, perhaps because of memories of living in various parts of the world with his diplomat father. He also generously gifted his original home to the Sisters of Mercy for their use with patients who had come to the area with tuberculosis and asthma and for the healing waters.

Francolon's mother, Marie, arrived in the United States in 1893, but set off immediately to travel. The priest moved into the mostly finished castle in 1896, and Marie moved into the completed east wing of the castle in early 1897. The castle rooms were sumptuous and the furnishings very elegant, as indicated by Marie's bed once belonging to Josephine. Marie had brought with her a bejeweled table and a hanging carpet, reported to have been made for an Egyptian king.

Despite Father Francolon's evidence of wealth, there were paradoxical occurrences that seemed rather peculiar. The Gillis Brothers, creators of his dream home, were later forced to take him to court to be paid for their labor. On the other hand, the Father was the soul of generosity, having endowed the Sisters of Mercy with his old home, and twice opening his lavish castle to the elite of the city for charity events to underwrite a local public library.

Then suddenly they were gone. In 1900, Francolon and his mother left quite abruptly, and it is believed that Mrs. Francolon died a few months later in France. Father Francolon disappeared for years, not emerging until his will was offered for probate in New York in late1922, indicating that he had died there.

Fourth floor gift store, once the servants' quarters.

SCANDAL

Perusing a book titled *Journeys,* the story of The Sisters of Mercy written by Kathleen O'Brien, one finds an account of the departure of Father Francolon in 1900. The Mother Superior, Mother Baptist, harshly accused the Father of accosting children. She then threatened to expose him. In response, the Father cursed her, telling her that she would be dead within a year's time.

Apparently the accusation reached the public ear and Angus Gillis, driving a wagon in town, came across an angry crowd headed for the castle. Driving ahead, Angus warned the Father, secreted him under a blanket in his wagon, and drove him to Colorado Springs where Father Francolon left abruptly for Europe.

A sad and creepy postscript to this tale is that in August of 1901, the very next year, Mother Baptist died quite horribly in a train accident while traveling from Durango to Silverton.

A less substantiated incident is that of a nun, Henrietta, who hanged herself, supposedly because she was carrying the child of Father Francolon, who refused to give up his priesthood and marry her.

Big time. It seems that Sister Henrietta never left and is still seen occasionally. There also is a little girl on the fourth floor, but who she is remains a mystery, although one psychic thought she might have been a patient who died there. A transparent Victorian couple has been seen on the grand staircase, once by the president of the Manitou Historical Society, and a Victorian widow sometimes appears in the mirrors in the mother's room. A Native American is another regular visitor.

Phenomena are so common that there are books on the third level for visitors to relate any odd occurrences that they encounter. And the entries are many. However, I noted that many are not sightings but are auditory and sensory experiences of footsteps on empty stairs or cold spots in closed rooms. This castle does seem a most appropriate place for a haunting, given its past.

ACCESS

Miramont Castle is open Tuesday through Sunday from 10:00 A. M. until 5:00 P. M. in the summer and 10:00 A. M. to 4:00 P. M. after Labor Day. Queen's Parlor Tearoom is open Tuesday through Saturday. Please see the Guide Sheet for details of the tearoom. Entrance to the castle ranges from $6.00 to free for children under five. Contact them by e-mail at: Miramontcastle@msn.com or call (719) 685-1011.

DIRECTIONS: I-25 to Exit 141 and Hwy 24. Follow the highway west several miles to the Manitou exit. Circle right and continue west on Manitou Blvd. almost through town to Ruxton Ave. Turn left up Capitol Hill to the banner, Miramont Castle. Then turn right.

BEULAH

Bishop's Castle

It's the only REAL castle in the world." Jim Bishop is leaning on a shovel in front of a concrete mixer. His weekends are now spent adding large rocks to a wall that will surround this acreage and cradle his masterpiece rising 160 feet above us—a castle composed entirely of stone, mortar, and ironwork—and created solely from *his* labor and design.

"It's been under siege ever since I first started it in 1969." For an avid anti-government citizen who's suffered pretty severely under pressure from the state and federal governments, he's remarkably calm. But then, it does seem as if he's won his battles—maybe even the war, as his creation soars up over one hundred feet above what the county allows. And what other castle can boast its own fire-breathing dragon?

Bishop's Castle begins twelve feet below the surface of the ground on bedrock. It stands on four sturdy flying-buttress legs, and rises three levels up to a large, A-frame great hall. Gothic windows on the front side provide light through clear glass with an occasional stained-glass hanging. An entire wall of small stained-glass panels is on the far end, individually donated and dedicated to the living and dead. When looking up from the great hall, the metal of the vaulted ceiling climaxes with a long glass window running the length of the top ridge so the viewer can look out to see the sky, the towers, and the ornamental metalwork bridges at

Great Hall

the rear of the castle. The sensation is that of being in a chapel without pews. Yet, looking up through the glass ceiling to the front end of the building, I can behold the dragon. Or at least the front end of it—the part that breathes fire. It's positioned at the tip of the great hall eighty feet in the air, and exhales flame with the aid of a propane burner taken from a hot air balloon (on weekends, usually).

All "real" castles need "keeps," or towers. Jim built his towers with internal staircases rising at each side of the back walls. The one on the left is

Top: weekend warrior. Bottom: Pa's Tower and bridge

Top: Unfinished bridge with a choice of a ladder going up or a rope going down.
Bottom: golden onion dome

the square tower, topped with a spire of ironwork taking its ultimate height to one hundred and sixty feet. This is the Roy Tower, named after a child they lost. Heavy stone steps firmly cemented into the walls spiral up from the great hall to a platform where you can oversee the entire area. Leaving the great hall to the right will take you up to the round "Pa" Tower, honoring Jim's father, Willard. Both towers, or chimneys, are capped with sculptures pointing in four directions. The Pa Tower doesn't stand as high as the Roy, but a metal bridge is in the process of connecting the two, for those free from altophobia. And holy

smoke, we're one hundred feet up, and you can see *through* this sucker. Currently, for anyone brave enough to cross the bridge, there is a choice of a ladder up, or a knotted rope down. It really brings home the reality of Jim Bishop monkey-scampering up and down this entire structure, and toting, at the least, tools, if not rocks and mortar. More amazing, this structure was built without plans, except in the mind of the builder.

An artistic addition high on the left front of the castle is a golden onion dome topping a small tower like a touch of the Kremlin. It looks as if it could be made of a delicate cloth, but it too is steel. Look around and you'll find four more in miniature decorating another tower.

To date, Jim has calculated using some 47,000 tons of assorted concrete, rocks, wood, and iron, and touching each rock at least six times. It boggles the mind to imagine one man hauling rock and concrete up to these heights, as Jim did, working only with pulleys, ropes, and a lift on rails that runs partially up the west side. A cement mixer built by his father in the 1950s has mixed all the mortar. None of the stonework is enclosed, so most of the work is done in the summer and on weekends, particularly since wet concrete just doesn't set up if it freezes. This castle is, quite literally, a monumental work.

The structure is unquestionably Colorado's most elaborate and imaginative piece of folk art. (Arguably the "most" elaborate in the entire United States or further.) Additionally, there is a gracefulness about it that is quite unusual in this genre, from the sweeping design of the legs and its graceful arches, to the elegance of its decorative ironworks that create the outer stairways and bridges and the inner roof support trusses. As Jim's sign says, the castle is "Built by One Man with the Help of God." He's also dedicated his castle to the independent individual who will stand up for his God-given rights.

HISTORY OF THE CASTLE AND JIM BISHOP

Most castles have had a major creator and then many owners, but not in this case. It's all Jim's. Jim has loved the mountains and woods all of his life. As a fifteen year old, he would ride his bike from his home in Pueblo into the San Isabel National Forest, often camping there with family or friends. One day, they came across a two-and-a-half acre lot for sale at the crest of a hill at 9,000 feet. His parents had to sign for it, as Jim was underage, but it was Jim's money that made the down payment, saved from mowing lawns, delivering newspapers, and working with his father Willard in the family ornamental iron works. The balance he took care of in monthly payments.

After quitting school at the tender age of fifteen, Jim worked for his father, learning the subtleties of working with ornamental iron. Not only did this provide Jim with a living, this true art form was to permeate his life. The Bishop family cleared and camped on the property until 1967, when Jim met and married his sweetheart Pheobe. With a portion of the land cleared, Jim gathered rocks and began to build a one room stone cottage for their home. Getting water to the cottage was a problem, so father Willard brought up a giant holding tank and surrounded it with rock.

The "Roy" Tower

Friends and neighbors often dropped by to watch the progress, and the rock enclosed water tank did indeed resemble a tower. "Looks like you're building a castle, Jim," he kept hearing over and over. This constant reference to the new structure as "Bishop's Castle" soon infected Jim's imagination, and so it was that a castle became the building's destiny.

PROBLEMS

One year after Jim started his construction, Custer County adopted building regulations. But the county waited for nine years and the Roy Tower was already 160 feet high, when they told Jim that he had to keep his structures 25 feet or less in height— a very uncastle-like requirement. Jim claimed and later proved that his rights were grandfathered in, therefore there were no limits to the height or composition of his castle. The government, very irked by someone able to function outside of their rules, tried another tack. Because Jim's land is located in a national forest, the government claimed that the rocks and trees he was using for construction belonged to it. Therefore, he could buy them for $16 a ton—prohibitive to someone with limited income. Fighting back, he whittled the cost down to fifty cents for several years. And even better, he eventually reached an agreement to pay $124 per year for all the rock he can use. But that was just one of many battles to come.

Now, in marched the IRS, stalking the revenue. Jim charges nothing to visit the castle, however, there are donation boxes and the government wanted its share. Pheobe did the legwork and the research, spending nights going over tax laws. The Bishop Castle Corporation, a nonprofit, was formed. Now 25 percent of the donations go to the Bishop Castle Foundation for Newborn Heart Surgery, and the castle is tax-exempt in a truly win-win situation.

ADDITIONS

Of course, there's the birth of the dragon. In the mid 1980s, a friend was driving discarded stainless steel warming plates to the dump one day, but figured that the Bishop Ornamental Iron Shop would be a better choice. Jim spent the winter

building a chimney out of the steel, riveting thousands of hammered "scales" together, which he'd cut out of the warming plates, and placed the scales around a steel frame for the head. In spring, the dragon was trucked to the castle and hoisted 80 feet in the air using pulleys and a truck, where it now rests at the top of the great hall, breathing fire on weekends.

Eventually, Jim plans to have a gatehouse and drawbridge, because, after all, this is a real castle.

There is also a gift shop on the property, selling castle shirts and renaissance items. The store was begun by Pheobe but is now run by other personnel.

Bishop's Castle is a Colorado treasure, and known to just about any native or visitor who has traveled the state to locate our obscure gemstones. Yet, several of the visitors at the castle when I came by were foreigners, so word is spreading. And besides having been a featured article in several magazines and newspapers, as well as a PBS special, Jim Bishop's castle has recently been listed in an English publication, *Destination Art*, by Amy Dempsey of the Tate Modern Museum of Art, as one of the two hundred most amazing structures in the world.

The castle is freely open to all. Any money spent there is either in the form of a donation or a purchase in the gift shop. No lighting is provided, so the castle is only open from dawn until sunset. It is posted ubiquitously, and generally understood, that when one enters the area or climbs to the various levels, the liability is ones own. The structure is surprisingly stable, with no tremors or vibrations wherever I went. Give me this castle over the Leaning Tower of Pisa any time.

My last visit was in a pouring rain, but it didn't seem to dampen the spirits of anyone there, and there were quite a few. The camaraderie warmed the spirit, and I saw not one incidence of rudeness, inconsideration, or impatience. We all shared our fears of ascending the high tower, or of walking the outer iron walkways and standing level with the dragon above the tops of the trees. We shared our awe, some even memories, of this man galloping around, creating this piece of folk art at dizzying heights, and of the beauty of the stained-glass windows, each a dedication to something or someone.

I left in the beating rain, and still people were coming, huddled under coats, helmets, or umbrellas, and slogging through the mud. They were, we were, there to participate in this alive and growing piece of art. How rare is that?

You can find Jim at work on almost any weekend before it gets cold. He's very approachable and informative. I guess after forty years, he's not too much in a hurry.

SCANDALS

"That government is best which governs least." This piece of wisdom from a philosopher of the past is succinctly that of Jim Bishop in the present. Jim's core belief is that freedom is an individual responsibility, and that if we were truly free people (which we are not, as soon as we receive a social security number, Jim says), we would really learn to govern ourselves.

Custer County officials are disturbed that the castle has sponsored, or allowed, Heavy Metal concerts and Rave parties. While neigh-bors have complained about the noise and traffic, Jim feels he's providing a safe place for young people to congregate.

ACCESS

The castle is open to the public at all times during daylight hours at no charge seven days a week, year-round, with only a request for a donation to help with Jim's costs for materials and to share in his charity.

DIRECTIONS: Past Pueblo off I-25. Take exit 74 (Colorado City), west past Rye and Lake Isabel into the mountains on CO Hwy 165. Drive for 24 miles and stop at the top of the ridge with the other parked cars.

ANTONITO

Cano's Castle

THE CASTLE TODAY

From a distance, they look like pure silver in the sun—two towers reflecting light even on an overcast day. Up close, they are made of the fabric of all folk art: stuff that would otherwise be rubble, trash, and throw-away. The gleam is from flattened aluminum cans and hub caps set in the rock and mortar that comprise the towers. And Cano, their creator, has explained them to me.

On the left, the taller of the two, is the King's Tower dedicated to Jesus and titled "Jesus Cristo." Its four stories are topped by an antenna with drooping arms, to replicate the body of Christ on the cross. On the right is the Queen Tower, dedicated to the Virgin Mary, and not quite as high. Both towers are studded with multiple windows, which in turn are decorated with the bright, shiny, smashed ends of one-time cans. Inscriptions of dedication to "La Virgin de Guadalupe" or a proclamation of "El Castillo" (The Castle) are written in rope at various levels. Padlocks are on the doors, and although I asked to see the interior, my request was either brushed off or disregarded. The towers, although some thirty feet high, are only eight to twelve feet in diameter, so it didn't seem important anyway.

It is obvious that Cano is a religious man. His yard holds three of his grandmother's religious statues of Mary, and a fourth, a small replica,

All castles have walls as barricades. And it's crenelated!

stands on a pedestal before the Queen Tower. It's interesting that these truly strange pieces of folk-art, built by one man with just the materials around him, seem to be attaining some sort of fame in the state.

HISTORY OF THE CASTLE

"Potatoes. It was the potatoes." This was the answer I got when I asked him why he had built his castle. Further explanation was that he used to harvest potatoes and truck them home, storing them in his house, until he'd filled the basement, closets, and all extra space. This led to his building a cellar, and later a steam room (his words) that became the base of his original tower. The second story was at first a "party room," and maybe this was the pivotal point.

Rumor has it that Cano was asked to clean up the cans in his yard. A seasoned builder, having built his own home, he began the first tower in 1980 over a small building that stood behind the house—his cellar. Reinforcing the roof, he created a second story with mortar and rock, embedding it decoratively with the ends of cans and using the tin for plating. By the time he built the third story, Cano had decided to dedicate the tower to Jesus, and had christened it the "Jesus Christ Castle." The construction of the first tower took over twenty years, and the second, begun in 1999, took seven years. How he has managed to work on the heights without equipment is perplexing, but he claims that they aren't finished yet.

CANO

Antonito is a small town, a village really. Still, I had wondered if I could find the piece of folk art known as Cano's Castle. Two towers of blazing silver caught the sunlight as I drove into town. Eureka. No problem there, but what now? The house in the yard of the towers had no doorbell, and its yard had a stone wall and iron gate. Then I saw a truck pull up.

"Cano, we have food for your goat." Two ladies in an old Ford 150 pulled up next to the patchwork two-story house right after I did. Yes, this was the place. And Cano, who called back to them, was at home. I had worried about finding both the castle and its creator, but here they both were.

"I love goats," I told the ladies, tagging along. (True statement.) And so I met Cano, a lean, rather small and soft-spoken man with skin the color of tanned leather.

I'd come about his castle, I explained. But he had family matters to attend to first. Cano, his niece, and I went up the open stairs to his living quarters (hang on to the rope and be careful). With an arm over her shoulder, he handed her $150 in small bills for clothes and school books, and to see a doctor about her headaches. That must have been grocery money for a month, I thought. He wanted her educated so she could "get out of here."

Cano is a decorated veteran of Vietnam. After spending a year in the front lines and receiving the Combat Infantry Badge award and the Army Accommodation with a V for valor, he was sent back to the United States and took four "extra" days to relax. The army counted him AWOL and dismissed him with no designation on his DD214,

which deleted any benefits the government offers veterans. It didn't help either, that in 1970 he joined those protesting the war. And it pulled no weight at all that both his father and uncle had been given medals of valor in World War II.

His given name is Dominic Espinosa, but he'd almost seemed to have forgotten it, as no one calls him anything but Cano. His ancestors were Indian—he named several tribes—and of course from Mexico, as his surname indicates. Cano has picked potatoes since he was in first grade. One of thirteen children, he was raised by his mother, since his father, after returning from the war, had an alcohol problem.

The land around, he feels, has been misused by ignoring God's Law of Seven, that is, grow crops for six years and let the land lie fallow for one. Confessing that I didn't know that, he murmured, "Ah, you're not a farmer."

Cano gave me some history of this area, where the Espinosas at one time had vast amounts of land, but were dispossessed by others coming in. This land does seem to be from another era. The number one language here is Spanish, and many families can trace their ancestry to the time when Colorado was not a state; even to pre-Louisiana Purchase. (Oral history, of course.) I found the customs here a bit exotic. With positive evidence of a resident horse in the yard, but no animal, I was told he was wandering the streets and lots, "free range." Also, his goat was down

about two blocks in a vacant lot. It seemed to be quite acceptable, as I passed other animals "free-ranging."

Cano claims his "castle" to be a work in progress, although I can't imagine what kinds of additions could be made. I guess I'll just have to wait and see. Maybe Joseph will get a turn too.

ACCESS
Drive due south from Alamosa and look left when entering Antonito.

FOOTHILLS

Castle Eyrie

One word we don't usually associate with a castle is the word "cozy," but this one is just that. The castle rooms, commonly massive, have been replaced with areas that seem more people-sized, even though the castle contains some 6,200 square feet. Although the elegance is there, this home is much more of a show of personal good taste and warm memories than opulence.

The two-story castle was built in the Colorado foothills of native stone around 1880 by Thomas Bryan, of British heritage, and was a recreation of the family home in England with the usual towers and crenelation. Its windows, though, are of special interest, as the structure was built by Chinese laborers who added unique trim on the doors and windows to welcome good spirits and keep out the evil ones. Surprisingly, almost all of the window glass is still original. The present owner has castle-ized it even more by adding a small moat and static drawbridge presided over by stone lions in front of the entrance. A variety of plants, shrubs, and trees sequester the site.

Inside, the front room is dominated by a fireplace of great timbers, uncarved but topped by a medallion of the family crest. The tower, off the corner of the room, is the source of the classical music playing throughout the home. To the left of the entry is a relaxing and casual den with a T.V. and books—an area set off from the rest of the house for desired quiet time. Although its décor is

with heads of American game animals, it is nonetheless called the Safari Room.

The largest room on the first floor is the library/music room, where the walls are paneled in wood from ancient cedar trees brought from Bryan's forest acreage in British Columbia. This many-sided room was originally for dining, but now holds books and a grand piano.

Off the dining room is the modern kitchen, small but with a wonderful, high ceiling. Here, the owner has left the original ceiling joists exposed, showing them "chamfered," or finished with a beveled edge—an architectural feature giving the narrow joists a very finished look. This high, open-beamed ceiling extends above the dining room as well, but at present, the dining room ceiling has been lowered, with wide black beams once salvaged from an exhausted mine stretching the length. The beams, along with the dark cedar paneling, create an intimate atmosphere where the focus is the candlelight reflecting on crystal and silver. In Bryan's time, the kitchen and dining room were one large ballroom, where the governor spent many a gala evening. It's reported that Buffalo Bill Cody attended his final party and dance here. Entry from the ballroom into the dining room then was through giant pocket doors, which now have been replaced with a solid wall.

In contrast to this dark interior, a Moorish solarium off the music room is styled with rounded windows pouring in light to a multitude of plants. The second story of this castle holds several bedrooms, much as they were in the past, where walls came and went, as the castle was turned into apartments and then restored by its present owner.

HISTORY OF THE CASTLE

Thomas B. Bryan, a lawyer, came to Colorado as an investor in gold mines, and was involved in tunnel construction and real estate as well. In the late 1870s he commissioned a structure for his daughter reminiscent of their English heritage—a castle was to be built of native stone with the requisite towers and crenelation using the labor of Chinese gold mine workers. Bryan owned vast areas of forest in British Columbia, and from there he got his lumber. The timbers for the castle were cut from old cedar forests and brought, first by rail and later ox-cart. The granite was all local rock.

Bryan and his family lived in the castle only three years before it was sold to the first of many

The castle just after completion, circa 1880.

owners. As could be expected, most if not many, of the new owners were not as well off as Bryan had been, and some strange tales can be told of its history. One owner, an Irishman of little means, ran a junkyard, collecting metal and reselling it for a small profit. Purportedly, children would sometimes steal items from his yard, and sell them back to him to finance their movie or candy bar. However, his high point came when he sold a set of tiles to top the Teller House in Central City.

Another era was most probably the castle's low point, when it's said that burros would wander in and out the apparently door-less castle. And later, in its apartment days, a sign was painted on the rocks in front announcing "Rooms for $1 a day." This may have been high living for a miner.

When it was bought by the present owner in 1965, it was understandably a sadly neglected and run-down building. Over the years, and using pictures from the past, the present owner has remolded the castle into the stately and warm home that it is presently.

THOMAS B. BRYAN

Because of a plaque, I was able to establish Thomas Bryan as the builder and creator of this castle, and several articles in the Georgetown

Colorado Miner newspaper indicated that this man was: 1) a governor, 2) mayor of Idaho Springs, and 3) of English peerage with a castle in his home country. All these inferences indicate a person of importance and means, as he owned many acres of forest in British Columbia. Yet it was hard to find references to him except for the few short years he was mayor of Idaho Springs. I

did later discover that Thomas Barbour Bryan was born in 1828 (no indication of where he was born) and died in 1906.

Cruising the Internet for his personal information, I learned of a Bryan family with many Thomases, who were descendents of Edward III, and therefore members of the British peerage of nobles. This would account for the family

homestead of a castle, and the ability of Bryan to purchase and hold large acreages of timberland in Canada.

From the *Colorado Miner*, dated October 16, 1880, I found this: "On the general election day votes will be cast for the head of the municipal government, to fill the vacancy caused by the resignation of Governor Bryan." Colorado never had a governor named Bryan, nor did any other state. An article in the May, 1920 edition of *Trail* explained that he was called "governor"

because he had once been a commissioner of the District of Columbia. This tied him in to our federal government.

His family is often written about in the *Colorado Mining Gazette* revealing that he had a wife, a son, Charles Page Bryan, and a daughter, "Miss Bryan." Her first name is never mentioned. Son Charles remained in Colorado and became a member of the legislature and later a diplomat to China. And this rather startling quote from the November 3, 1883 *Gazette*: "Miss May Lee,

daughter of General Robert E. Lee, will be a guest of her cousin, Miss Bryan . . ." Poor "Miss Bryan." I wonder if her first name was "Miss."

Bryan claims to have been pressed into taking the office of mayor. However during the two years that he held the office he accomplished three goals: he saw that the train depot was moved from the center of town, he codified and printed the ordinances "which were in inaccessible shape" into book form, and most important, saw that water was piped into the town of Idaho Springs. These had been his goals, and when attained, he voluntarily resigned his office. Bryan also built a bathhouse, hoping to furnish it with water from the natural hot springs nearby, but this resulted in a lawsuit which he lost. He then moved to Chicago from the area in 1883.

SCANDAL

One article dated May 28, 1881, gave an explanation of the lawsuit re: Governor/Mayor Bryan. "Governor Bryan has laid the foundation of the large bath house … and is tunneling and sinking for the water that is to supply the bath."

This area of Idaho Springs is located on a hot springs, which had been run for years by a popular citizen of the town, and purportedly used by such luminaries as Frank and Jesse James, Walt Whitman, Horace Tabor, and Sarah Bernhardt. By claiming to mine for gold while actually tapping into the sulfur springs, Bryan was essentially stealing another man's livelihood. There followed a lawsuit in which Bryan was the loser.

HAUNTED

The present owner has not run across "her," but a guest at dinner, a prominent and quite well-known painter, did see and hear a figure in the dining room one evening, who told him her name was Mary. Adjourning to the solarium for coffee, the guest saw her there as well. Other guests have felt cool breezes in the music room, with no open doors or windows. Mary is possibly the daughter of Bryan, but that remains an unverified fact.

ACCESS
None

NEAR CONIFER

Hardin Castle

THE CASTLE TODAY

From childhood we've all known that to reach a fairy tale castle, one must approach it by trekking up a winding road on a precipitous mountain, which will culminate in a dramatic and glamorous fortification on a rocky pinnacle or "tor." Cautiously, we followed the torturous climb through the forest and up, until, sure enough, there it is—a real one—stone turrets and all.

Looking straight up, the towers of yellow limestone rise a good fifty feet, while carved stone angel faces look down on us as we approach. It's a dozen steep stone steps up to the massive Miranda mahogany door, and walking through, we're standing on a bare concrete floor in a large open space with monstrous rocks in the rear; scattered construction equipment is its only furnishing. But a wide, curved staircase of rich walnut pulls my eyes up to the second level, which is well lit and edged by a matching walnut railing. The upper living space looks inviting.

"Come on up," I hear. At the top we're in a great room dominated by a huge, carved, stone fireplace. Lining the walls on either side are arched windows giving a view of 180 degrees, overlooking forest and small farms. A posh sofa faces the fireplace, and on the floor is planking of the ubiquitous walnut. Here is an elegant living space that Meme (Mimi) and Doc Hardin have created out of a shell. Meme shows us around.

A lion at the gate

The fireplace is of conterra stone and volcanic rock, harvested and handcarved in Mexico. Very fond of Gothic design, Meme mimicked a seventeeth century style, having acanthus leaves carved in the stone across the top. The mantel was then hauled up in four pieces, each block weighing 400 pounds. The Roman arch windows are German-made and tilt-turn, opening from the top or the side. In fact, all windows in the house have been imported from Germany. Ten feet above and stretching across the great open space over the entry are I-beams nattily dressed in dark alder. The ceiling then is a rich criss-cross of wooden beams with medallions at the junctions—warm brown skin with a skeleton of steel—spanning this great room and the cave-like entry below.

Marble-floored dining room

Down several steps to one side is the dining area with a marble floor, complete with a rectangular marble inlay in place of an area rug. The formal dining table is adjacent to a fireplace, open on both sides and built through a conterra stone wall that divides the dining room from Doc's sports bar. At the far end is the kitchen where the marble floor continues. Nothing the fussiest gourmand could want is missing here, from the polished granite countertops to various ovens here and there and an island for coffee that would turn Starbucks green with envy. Cooking a Thanksgiving dinner would be a piece of cake here, I think.

Outside the kitchen looking south is a balcony lined with hummingbird feeders. Although filled daily, one feeder is sucked dry while birds seem to be waiting in line for their turns at the other stations. It's almost like standing in front of a bee hive with some fifty or more Ruby-throats zooming, scrapping, and eating, at Star Wars speed. One syntillating orange bird stands out—a rare Rufus, I'm told. Off the balcony, an orange fox scoots out of a lower rock pile, the mother of a litter. The wildlife here is replete with raccoons, elk, fox, bear, and even a mountain lion.

Going west out of the great room is Doc's office, abundantly supplied with ducks, and hunting equipment. A retired physician (surprise!), his office has a wall covered with one of the few pieces of furniture that was salvaged with the house, an apothecary cabinet with dozens of small drawers. Meme supplied new brass handles and the cabinet, now refinished, looks new. Doc has planned and supervised most of the electrical wiring, and there are intricate systems throughout, including radiant heat in the floors. The wiring includes several exterior cameras, as I think they've had an overdose of uninvited visitors.

Doc's office is just ducky, and I'm being quite literal. He and Meme are both very involved with an organization called Ducks Unlimited, begun in the 1930s to conserve the continent's wetlands. The burgeoning of population and development has resulted in the depletion of wetland areas necessary for migrating birds. Finally in the 1930s, Mexico, Canada, and the United States created a foundation called Ducks

Doc's apothecary cabinets

Unlimited to preserve these vital areas. Doc now devotes a great deal of his time and effort in raising funds for it.

Down the hall is the posh and inviting master bedroom and attached bath. Meme has remodeled many houses in the past and has an unerring sense of design. Her original touch is everywhere as she fits together the unusual, resulting in many a pleasant surprise. And apparently her friends just expect this, as one time a guest interpreted the ubiquitous bare light bulbs as her "feng shui," when actually the fixtures hadn't yet been delivered.

Most of the second level is finished, but the third level above is a work in progress as a studio

Ducks mounted in Doc's office

Roof cabana

for Meme and her large library, a bath, and more bedrooms. At the time of this printing, large areas had been dry-walled only, but with over 8,000 square feet of living space and with the taste and savoir faire afforded each room, this castle has the makings of the Parade of Homes on steroids. The third level has Meme's circular office in a front turret with a beamed ceiling in its party hat roof. It has loads of books and book shelves, and is a true "get away from it all."

More stairs lead to the open deck on the roof and the top of the world. The view from here is lit-erally 360 degrees. On a clear day you can see as far as the canvas peaks of DIA to Evergreen, north to Longs Peak, and as far south as Pikes Peak, as well as the many small hamlets dolloping the foothills. At an elevation of 9,000 feet, it may not be the highest point in Colorado, but it might as well be.

Additionally, off the garage on the lowest level is an elevator that can take you up four flights. And still to be added here below are a the-ater area, a wine cellar, a game room with pool table, and other big-kid toys. A major project in the future will be creating a waterfall over the

Top: Staircase from lower level
Above: kitchen

rocks in the "cave," around which Doc's electric train will run. Every castle should have one.

HISTORY OF THE CASTLE

These sixty acres containing the castle and grounds were apparently homesteaded by the Smedley family, and near the entrance off the highway is a small cabin where Mrs. Smedley, a writer, came for the peace and quiet.

The outer shell and basic inner structure of the castle was built in the early 1980s with a construction date listed as 1983. The second level held only stud walls, with the 2x4s dividing areas to indicate future rooms.

By 1996 the castle had been abandoned for several years, and though sturdy on the outside,

had been victim to what seemed to be every destructive teen and adult for miles around. Every window had been smashed, the shards of safety glass lay in dunes both inside and outside. The previous owners had stored both their parents' "stuff" and their own as well, and generations of baby clothes, furniture, toys, clothes, and used appliances were strewn throughout. Parties had been held there, as mountains of trash gave evidence, with one room waist deep in old clothing that had been torn out of boxes.

The Hardins bought the castle that same year and started work one year later, after clean-up and applying for permits were taken care of. The castle is a work in progress, but even now is a unique and progressive home.

THE HARDINS

When physician William Kendrick Hardin, or "Doc," planned to retire and give up his Louisiana practice, he asked wife Meme, "Where would you like to live?" and her answer was, "Why don't we

Hardin family crest

What a view!

live where we play?" The Hardins were skiers, fishermen, and outdoor people, and Colorado had been their playground, so the family moved to Evergreen—Meme, Doc, Bill Jr., age 11, Ivey, 12, and Grant, 10. It was an early retirement for Doc Hardin, but an accident while deer hunting had laid him up, and Doc was ready for a change.

Evergreen was a nice place, but not exactly what they wanted. "Exactly," in fact, was a spread in the mountains surrounded by wildlife and preferably with a view. Something in the raw would be fine, as Meme, with a degree in Fine Arts, the owner of Margaret Hardin Design, and a veteran of many a project of restoration and remodel, was ripe for a new challenge. In stepped Kismet.

Their appraiser friend warned them ahead of time, but the mess in front of the castle was so bad, Doc refused to leave the car. The poor castle seemed to vomit refuse, from baby beds to old clothing, mattresses, and every sort of human leftovers. Wading cautiously up the front stairs and through the front door, Meme and their appraiser took in the entire scene, up and down. Only the subflooring had been laid, and it was rotting from snowfall that had drifted through the broken windows. Trash was everywhere, and the remains of several pieces of antique furniture that had been left were burned in the fireplace. It seemed an impossible challenge.

However, the friend made an appraisal with all positives and negatives accounted for, and came up with a figure. They then got together with the owner who, when presented with the offer, quite literally laughed in their faces. One must not be rude to a southern belle, as he found out later. Circumstances put the seller in a position of must-sell, and they lowered their offer.

The Hardins started work immediately but the vandalism continued. Alarms were set up throughout the castle to alert the sheriff, who, every weekend would ring them up to tell them that someone was in the castle. One couple tore out a new front door, frame and all, so they could sit on the upper deck and "gaze at the stars." This couple did end up paying for the replacement, under protest. Those stars they were gazing at must have been lucky ones, since Doc could have had them prosecuted for breaking and entering.

A garage, termed carriage house, had been built below the castle hill, and Meme turned it into their temporary home. But moving from Evergreen into the carriage house didn't stop intruders, nor did the alarm system or the many calls to the sheriff. Another final incident was Doc's blocking the road one day with his truck, trapping the kids—found with pot in their car—who were prosecuted. Finally, moving into the castle itself, the Hardins enclosed most of the sixty acres with a fence and an electronic gate. That seemed to finally put an end to the invasion.

Obviously, the Hardins are something special. While she was in college, Meme spent time in Raton, South America, doing missionary work. While they were living in Evergreen, a friend of Doc's involved them both on a mission to build a church for Methodist Panamanians on a small island off Panama. They've taken two two-week sojourns to live and work under brutally primitive conditions. Meme tells of the boat trips out over piranha-infested waters in a leaky, low dinghy with no life jackets. "If you fall in," their translator stated, "you don't want to float. Better to go all at once." Yuk. But it was the snakes that seemed to be the bigger problem, as they were everywhere. Yes, they'll go again.

Doc devotes much of his time and energy to Ducks Unlimited and is the District Manager for southwest Denver, which apparently covers the foothills area as well. Meme is almost as involved as he is, and they orchestrate banquets, raffles, art sales, and various money-raising events to finance the purchase of wetlands, not only for birds but as habitat for deer, raccoons, and other wildlife that are vital to our ecosystem.

Today, the castle is not yet complete, but promises to be a true showplace as well as an asset to our state. True lovers of the land, the Hardins care for their land as a tree farm, removing underbrush and dead trees—clearing away debris that feeds forest fires. That's quite a job on sixty acres. One son has his own contracting business, and has contributed, but both Hardins are hands-on workers, and value the people who have worked with them.

And when it's done, will there be more projects? Meme just smiles.

ACCESS
Sorry, but no. This is a private home.

WOODLAND PARK

The Lion and the
Rose Castle

THE CASTLE TODAY

Some dreamers dream, and some dreamers build. After sopping up the mystique of the European aristocracy once living in the sullen castles of England, France and Germany, one couple has built their own Shangri-la in the sunny foothills of Colorado above Woodland Park. Lording over twenty wooded acres atop its own "motte," the castle has three towers as well as decorative, crenelated gables, and it backs up to over a million acres of protected national forest. The view from the towers would satisfy any potentate, as one can see in 360 degrees—from the hilly plains to the east, and south to Pikes Peak, the Rampart Range, and Devil's Head rock formation. The view to the west takes in the snowcapped peaks of Mount Bierstat and Mount Evans. It is romantically called The Lion and the Rose Castle, the name honoring the owners' favorite animal, the cat, and their favorite flower, the red rose. Its 8,726 square feet were originally used as a bed and breakfast, but now serve as a very private home, which the couple has furnished with numerous antiques collected during their travels.

The waterfall outside the entrance is a refreshing idea in this dry country. Water falls fifteen feet over heavy granite boulders into three ponds, all connected by a flowing stream. To enter the castle, one must cross the stream on a stone bridge and pass through a heavy Gothic front door into an airlock flanked by cast marble pillars.

Waterfall outside the entrance of the castle.

Gigantic chandelier of Austrian crystal hangs twenty feet in the air.

From here the ascent is up to the great hall, a room dominated by a cast marble fountain spouting water from a large lion head, which is mounted on the wall above it. From twenty feet above hangs a gigantic chandelier of Austrian crystal. This huge room holds antique Victorian furniture, and the moldings around the room are finished with a paint embedded with flecks of real gold. In fact, most of the woodwork in the castle glows with this special gold paint, including door frames, window frames, some chandeliers, picture frames, and crown moldings. It's rather overwhelming elegance. This is a style of French Baroque seldom seen since the days of the Louis's.

Moldings are finished with paint embedded with flecks of real gold.

Doré clock with matching candelabra.

But even Marie Antoinette would envy the comfort found here. If the day is cool, the Italian marble floor under your feet will be warmed by radiant hot-water heat. This in-floor heating system runs throughout both the main and upper levels, covering over 4,900 square feet. Where carpeted, the pad itself is a special conductor. Wow.

Beyond the great hall is the parlor, dominated by a gold mantel against a wall of cerulean blue. It looks like a great place to sit back and gaze into a fire while listening to the grand piano being played in the next room. And "grand" piano is

Musical chandelier

right. The instrument is a stunning, nine-foot concert grand of rosewood, built in 1874. It's obvious that the people here are musical, for if the piano is quiet, the soothing sound of falling water is right outside the open window.

The dining room contains a unique musical chandelier dome, lined with satin, to serenade anyone eating a formal dinner here. The mantel in this room is of rare mahogany, elaborately carved as was common in that era, and topped with a doré clock flanked on either side with matching candelabra.

The castle was a bed and breakfast from 1996 until 2001, when the owners decided to retire the B&B to enjoy the five suites in the castle by themselves. Their master suite, appropriately titled the King's Suite, (Tiffany's Suite) is situated on the main level, its furnishings are luscious Victorian. But the favorite feature in this room is the great cast marble spa, which is flanked by electrified marble columns that glow at night. And from here, the view from the Tudor windows overlooks a vast kingdom of gentle, forested hills.

Top: Tiffany Suite; Above left: doré bronz rococo-style clock, circe 1820; Above right: Cast marble fountain

The Lion Suite is furnished in gold and green, with an elaborate bed of brass resting on plush carpet in a room replete with paintings of lions. Dominating the Rose Suite is a huge headboard of elaborately carved American walnut ten feet tall—nearly reaching the ceiling. This piece, along with its matching dresser, was made in 1860, as was the diamond dust mirror over the dresser, all set off by the reds and maroons of the room.

The castle has five suites in all, with four on the upper level, all five having private bathing facilities with music channeled in, but controlled room by room.

Below, in the lower level, is the theatre room with a flat screen HD TV and surround-sound, which can be channeled throughout the castle. Also on this level are two double-car garages, able to accommodate four cars comfortably.

As luscious as this castle may be, it is still a private dwelling, and is shared with us only in pictures. But it's proof that dreams *can* come true.

HISTORY OF THE CASTLE

Many couples traveling to Europe visit castles there, but this couple found themselves totally enchanted, to the point of wishing for their own realm. After returning home, they sought out and found an excellent and appropriate architect for their project, and construction was begun in 1992. You may have noted that many of the castles built in the late 1800s were innovative in design and by the use of the most advanced features of electricity and plumbing. This castle too, conceived and built some one hundred years later, over a period of five years, has incorporated the most innovative and appropriate materials for its construction.

The castle necessities of great hall, crenelation, and medieval design are there. But there was no gathering of native rock to create this castle. Here, the construction is concrete impregnated with fiberglass for unparalleled modern-day

Top: Built with concrete impregnated with fiberglass; Above: Two hundred tons of granite were used for landscaping.

structural integrity. The walls themselves are of R-30 insulation value, blown in with wool, and are seven-and-a-half inches thick, sufficient to ward off mountain snowstorms and firestorms as well. The massive roof tiles, also concrete, were made to withstand the intense hail so often found in the mountain areas; the concrete mixed not with water but with acrylic.

Landscaping, too, was a task for giants, with the hauling and placement of 200 tons of granite boulders, turned on end, to create a private Garden of the Gods.

If this sounds more like the Brooklyn Bridge than a dream home, the engineering here is subtly internal, with the aura of fairytale romance still intact. Kudos are due to the architect.

Dreamers often need outside help to crystallize their hopes. Nevertheless, the idea must come before the reality—the dream itself only the springboard and first step. The Lion and the Rose is quite literally a concrete example of a dream solidified. This tasteful mixture of the old and the brand new have created a completely unique living space for a very imaginative couple.

HAUNTED

These denizens, wandering in and out the castle without invitation, are not your usual spirit entities. These guys leave great disastrous messes, and footprints—rather, paw prints—so it isn't hard to determine that another raccoon has torn out the screen, reached in and rolled open the window, and helped himself to the pet food. Not once, mind you, but often.

Then there are the bigger guys. The couple has had five bear break-ins, and some heart-stopping, but now funny, moments. One time as the wife entered the kitchen, she saw a bear standing on the counter in the pantry, and hastily backing through the door, she scooted into the basement to come around and close the open basement door, thus hoping to trap the bear in the kitchen. As she was tip-toeing up to the landing, the bear, around a corner, was coming down, until, almost nose to nose, they frightened the bejesus out of each other, and each ran back the way he/she had come. The bear left the way he'd come in.

I would have had a double Scotch. She simply shrugged, saying that it was to be expected as they lived in the animals' territory, with the pet food an unintentional temptation.

And you thought it was all roses, living in a castle! Like I said, this is quite a special couple.

ACCESS
Nope. Private home

REDSTONE

Redstone Castle

THE CASTLE TODAY

If all castles were relatives in some way, the Redstone Castle would be the famous rich-kid cousin who had become the family black sheep. Born into magnificence and splendor, the castle has been draped in riches of velvet and gold, yet has also been neglected, abandoned, and misused. Poor little rich-castle.

The castle reopened to the public in June of 2007 following a turbulent decade in which it was seized and taken over by the IRS in 2003 during an investigation of an alleged multimillion dollar fraud scheme. Finally purchased at auction in 2005 for some four million dollars, its extensive upgrades are currently going on; still, five rooms inside the building and its exterior cannot be changed as they are covered by a State Historic Foundation easement. Of all the creations of stony magnificence in Colorado, this is perhaps the most opulent. Will its grandeur have endured this trip onto the dark side of life? The new owner promises that its future is bright.

The original structure was built between 1898 and 1901 by John Cleveland Osgood, a Colorado coal baron, at a cost of $2.5 million. Redstone Castle has forty-two large rooms and 24,000 square feet, and sits on seventy-two acres. Built in the style of a sixteenth-century Tudor castle, with towers, turrets, and oriel windows, it was begun for Osgood's first wife, Irene, but later finished and furnished for his adored second wife, Alma.

This dragon is also a fountain.

The exterior of the first and second story is of cut and coursed red sandstone, while the third story and gabled ends are covered with wood shingles, which are not all together castle-y. Ah, but inside—it's like opening an egg by Fabergé.

Throughout the castle the décor is of green and red, symbolic of wealth and royalty. The great hall has a massive fireplace over which is carved the Osgood coat of arms, showing a lion holding a sheaf of wheat—the symbol of free-born landed gentry. That it was borrowed from *another* Osgood family, no relative, never seemed to matter. The lion was the important factor, and lions can be found throughout the castle.

Each room in the castle adapts the style of a European country, and the great hall is strongly English. Oak paneling covers the walls, and the great Tiffany lamps hanging above the furnishings were actually owned and used by the Osgoods. A small aperture high up at the end of the great hall is a "peering" window, used by Alma up in her quarters, who determined what dress to wear by observing the costumes of her guests. Adjoining the great hall is the library, once called the Persian Room. The walls are covered with hand-tooled green elephant hide, and above this, a stunning frieze of hand-stenciled peacock tails, while overhead, the ceiling is pure half-inch-thick gold leaf. The warm dark wood here is Honduran mahogany.

The music room is definitely French. Overhead are delicate plaster frescoes with an intricate crystal chandelier as the centerpiece. This is a replicated replacement, as the original chandelier was stolen and later found in pieces. Surrounding us are wall

Top: Massive fireplace with the Osgood coat of arms.
Above: Tiffany lamps and "peering" window

coverings of green taffeta, which set off the diamond dust mirror that's atop a white marble fireplace.

The dining room, off the far side of the great hall, is the only interior room, and is decorated with head-high Honduran mahogany paneling with Russian velvet wall coverings above the paneling. An elaborately carved fireplace of dark mahogany is the centerpiece of the main wall. Perhaps all this rich darkness was intentional—to set off the Bavarian crystal and silverware. Off the dining area is the long loggia, as light a room as the dining room is dark. Oak is used for both floors and ceiling, and a dozen windows overlook the estate and the mountains beyond.

Intricate crystal chandelier in the music room

Great room furniture hosted the Osgoods.

The second level has eight bedrooms, all with baths, as it once, and maybe still will be, a bed and breakfast. The level above this is the nanny's room that has a stunning turreted ceiling wallpapered in trees and birds. To the back of this room and four steps down is a small bedroom for a child or children. An interesting fact here is that John Osgood himself never had any children.

Of course, the men had their own space in the lower level—a dungeonesque room with a large pool table.

The estate was built as a hunting lodge, and many animal heads remain as evidence. But Alma's touch is everywhere as well. Door handles

Top: Elaborately carved fireplace of dark mahogany in the dining room. Bottom: The Persian Room, or library.

Elegant and intimate dining

were all made by Tiffany, and the molds for them were later broken so they couldn't be reproduced anywhere else. Stone cutters from Austria and Italy adorned the exterior with their art, and the interior with exotic marble fireplaces. Tiffany chandeliers sparkle in rooms above lush Persian rugs that cover some, but not all, of the intricate inlaid wood patterns in the floors. The artwork on the walls is hand-painted and stenciled linen, and was commissioned by Alma, who imported Italian painters to do the interior décor.

Osgood had a bevy of ultra-wealthy friends, and he was obviously out to impress them. "Dropping in" were guests like Leopold, king of Belgium, J.P. Morgan, John D. Rockefeller, and Teddy Roosevelt. The buzz is that 75 percent of the original furnishings are still in place, and with the recent scandal and its solution, the docents now have an even more complex history to relate.

The castle, originally called Cleveholm Manor, was the baronial home of John and Alma Osgood, and part of a complex that included quarters for servants, a guard house, two gate houses, a greenhouse, a game keeper's house, and carriage house. Osgood was a patriarchal owner of a full-scale coal mining operation, creating an entire town for the benefit of his miners and their families, with his castle, known as the "Ruby of the Rockies," the palace of the king. And lavish it was, with fifteen bedrooms, eleven baths, a library, quarters for the maid, and a game room. Unusual for the times, it was furnished with electricity and plumbing. It had a wine cellar, a walk-in vault, an armory, and an elevator to reach the upper floor.

The Osgoods moved into the castle in 1901, and for three years tended the ideal but patriarchal society in the town of Redstone that Osgood had created. Alma was soon called Lady Bountiful for her devotion to the people and her egalitarian manner. In 1903 a labor strike embittered Osgood, ending the experimental town, and in 1909, Alma divorced him to marry an English nobleman. John was fifty-eight years old, while she was decades younger. Osgood closed the castle in 1913, and spent the next twelve years traveling in the eastern United States and Europe.

A rather odd occurrence happened during the twelve years that Osgood was gone. A woman claiming to be the wife of Osgood arrived at the castle and removed two boxcar-loads of furniture, art objects, rugs, and other valuables. She was supposed to have lived with Osgood for only a few months, but it was never verified whether or not they were married. Later it was also discovered that much of the silver and crystal was missing from the estate, though the castle had been kept under lock and key.

Osgood returned to the castle in 1925 with his third wife, Lucille, whom he had married two years prior. She was noted for her green thumb, growing prize-winning potatoes and lettuce. Like Alma, she did much for the townspeople. However, Osgood was ill with lung cancer, and died one year later at the age of seventy-five. The castle, with all personal property, profits from his four companies, and $4 million were all left to Lucille.

Lucille remarried in 1933, and she and her new husband tried to make the area a resort, but it was the time of the Great Depression, and they had little success. In the mid-1930s she sold off much of the adjacent properties, and ultimately sold the castle itself for $100,000.

In the 1950s the castle was bought by Frank Kistler, owner of the Hot Springs Pool in Glenwood Springs, with the intention of making the Redstone area a resort. He added an additional wing to the Redstone Inn, originally a hotel for Osgood's bachelor miners, and was responsible for building the enclosed swimming pool, a golf course on the front lawn, small ski lift, and tennis courts. He had the ambition to create a Sun Valley-like ski resort here in Colorado, but died before he could develop his idea. The castle was operated as a hotel well through the seventies, and later also as a dude ranch.

In the 1980s the castle was sold for $2.5 million, and became a bed and breakfast for the next seventeen years, while sponsoring retreats and wedding receptions.

In 1997 a developer bought the property with the idea of breaking it up into home sites, but this plan failed to materialize, and in 2000, it was purchased for $6.3 million by Leon and Debbie Harte. Within a year, the Hartes, along with several accomplices, were accused of running a brokerage firm selling worthless investments, and having purchased the castle with what was determined to be stolen money. In 2003, the Internal Revenue Service seized the castle along with sixty bank accounts, eight NASCAR race cars, and multiple assets amounting to around $24 million, a portion of which was to be returned to the investors to cover part of their losses.

The new owner is Ralli Dimitrius, of both Redondo Beach, California, and Aspen, Colorado. Bidding $4 million, he acquired the castle at auction in March of 2005, and is currently working on necessary repairs. The castle opened to the general public in June of 2007.

JOHN CLEVELAND OSGOOD

John Cleveland Osgood was born in Brooklyn in 1851, into a family with roots reaching back to the Colonial period. His cousin, Grover Cleveland, became the twenty-second president, and his great-uncle Moses Cleveland founded the city in Ohio bearing his name. John's mother died early in his life, and his father succumbed to a fever when John was seven, leaving him an orphan to live with some Quaker relatives. He was forced to leave school at age fourteen because of financial difficulties.

Stone cutters from Austria and Italy adorned the exterior with their art.

From what seemed like a pretty ominous beginning, John worked in menial jobs as an office boy and clerk, attending night school in New York, until he impressed an assistant treasurer of a Colorado coal company, A. D. Moss. Moss suggested nineteen-year-old John for a job as bookkeeper for the Union Mining Company of Ottumwa, Iowa, and it was this job that seemed to determine his goal in life. Convinced that coal held the riches of the future, he worked as a bank cashier and saved enough money to assume control of the financially troubled White Breast Mining Company. He was also clever at finance and managed to maintain control of the contract for being the major supplier of coal for the Chicago, Burlington, and Quincy railroads.

Osgood came to Colorado in 1882 at the age of thirty to scout for coal for his company. Legend has it that he was in the valley of Rock Creek, a creek he later renamed Crystal, when he came across two gold miners whose claim had been disturbed by a landslide. Much to the disappointment of the miners, the landslide uncovered coal, not gold. Disgusted, they sold the claim to Osgood for $500, who, after scraping together a partnership, bought it for himself. Osgood then formed the Colorado Fuel Company, and within two years, controlled seven hundred acres of coal land. Four years later his acreage was some 5,622, moving him to a very dominant position in the fuel trade. Even General William J. Palmer (see Glen Eyrie Castle), who owned a rival industry, the Colorado Coal and Iron Company, buckled under to the financially superior strength of Osgood's Colorado Fuel Company, allowing the companies to merge and Osgood to buy him out. This 1892 merger created the giant Colorado Fuel and Iron Company, better known as the C.F. and I., that within a decade, was the single largest employer in the state.

A year before the merger, Osgood had met and married a southern belle named Nannie Irene de Belote. Southern belle she may have been, but a Victorian lady she was certainly not. Irene was a writer of romantic novels, apparently more of the bodice-ripper type than those of mere flirtatious ingénues. Ten years younger than Osgood, she was more the coquette than committed wife.

In 1893 the miners had started to fight for better living conditions and to form a union, the United Mine Workers of America. Osgood was fully against the union, as were all the mine owners. The workers were caught up in slave-like conditions, having no legal rights, since supervisors, sheriffs, and officials were accountable to the mine owners. Any complaints were met with brutality or blacklisting, and the miner was usually paid with script rather than money, which could only be spent in the company store. Foreigners, unaware of the dire conditions, were recruited and shipped over from their homelands, so now the miners often worked with men they could not even verbally communicate with. In 1901, according to Sylvia Rutland in *The Lion of Redstone,* twenty-seven languages were represented in the mines of the C.F. and I.

With Irene's flirtatiousness and the miners' unrest, Osgood was between a rock and a hard place. By 1898 Osgood was discussing divorce with his personal lawyer and partner, J. L. Jerome. By then, Irene had run off with her future husband, Captain Pigott Harvey, after telling Osgood that she had no intention of moving to the wilderness (Colorado) with him. Horrified by the thought of scandal that a divorce would cause, Osgood reported to the *New York Times* that his wife had been killed by a runaway horse. And so it was reported.

By October of 1899, both had remarried, Irene to Harvey and Osgood to his second wife, Alma Regina Shelgrem, the beautiful future Lady Bountiful. She too had been married before, and for this reason, the stuffy Denver society comprised of the tightly knit "Sacred Thirty-Six," snubbed the new couple. It was unfortunate for Osgood's lawyer, J. L. Jerome, that Jerome's wife was part of that group, as Osgood held Jerome personally responsible for their alienation, although Jerome himself was quite egalitarian and not likely to have had any responsibility at all. Eventually, Jerome was financially destroyed, as Osgood ground him down, year by year.

To avoid unionization, Osgood decided to invoke a countermeasure. In 1889 he began to construct the town of Redstone. Each worker's family received a brand new house, individually painted in pastel colors, with a garden and fenced yard. All homes had running water and electricity, and each month the home judged to have the best yard was given a prize. For the single men, Osgood built the Redstone Inn and equipped it with a barber shop, electric lights, hot and cold water, a laundry, telephones, reading rooms, and steam heat. During the summer of 1901, he appointed Dr. Richard Corwin, head of C.F. and I's two-room hospital, to launch programs in five specific areas: education, social training, industrial training, housing, and communications. One of the state's first kindergartens was started under this plan. It was paternalism at its peak.

A clubhouse was built with a bar, lounge, game rooms, and a fully equipped theater, with ladies allowed in on Wednesday nights. It was here the men showered and left their dirty work clothes so none would be seen walking in coal-smothered clothing on the streets of the town. A library was built and stocked with books chosen by the Osgoods. Alma, now called Lady Bountiful by the miners, frequently drove her carriage through the town, talking with the townspeople and often attending to their needs.

Concerts were held in the summertime on the lawn of the castle for the benefit of the miners and their families. At Christmas time, Lady Bountiful went to New York and hand-picked four hundred gifts for the children of Redstone. No labor troubles existed during Redstone's idealistic three-year period, which lasted from 1899 until 1903. The company received an award for their village from the St. Louis Exposition of 1902, making what was probably Osgood's finest hour. Then in 1903, miners in nine of the C.F. and I. mines walked out in sympathy with miners elsewhere on strike, and the experiment was over.

That same year J. D. Rockefeller gained control of the C.F. and I. in a hostile takeover, and Osgood refused to merely be the chairman of the board. He took over another enterprise, the Victor and American Fuel Company, which he had secretly invested in, anticipating problems. Unfortunately for his friends, he had not included the three men who had partnered with him since he had begun his mining in Colorado, one being J. L. Jerome. All were left in the dust and financially ruined, and all three were dead before the year was out—one of a heart attack, one of a stroke, and Jerome's death was suicide.

In 1909 Lady Bountiful divorced Osgood to marry an English earl, and Cleveholm Manor was closed in 1913, as Osgood spent much time in the eastern part of the United States and Europe. He met his third wife, Lucille, while vacationing in Hot Springs, Arkansas. They were married in 1920—she was barely twenty-five and he was in his seventies. Being gravely ill, Osgood brought her back to the castle in 1925 and died one year later, leaving her the castle and grounds and all his substantial holdings. His ashes were scattered near the Crystal River.

SCANDAL

Rumor has it that Alma at one time may have had a love affair with one of the Italian artists she had imported to paint inside the mansion, and that Osgood had him shot for allegedly cheating in a poker game. No real evidence documents this story, however there is a secret passageway through the castle from the guest quarters, which comes out very near Alma's private suite.

The biggest black mark on Osgood's character was his reaction to the horrific Ludlow Massacre in 1914, where a camp of striking miners and their wives were gunned down and burned out by men in the employ of the mine owners. As spokesman for the coal operators of Colorado, he loquaciously blamed the victims for the problem, although he was fully aware of, and had participated in, the evil conditions the miners endured. Later testimony disproved his claims, but perhaps his sympathies had been blunted by the desertion of his adored wife, and later the betrayal of the miners in walking out of his mines.

HAUNTED

Most prevalent is the smell of cigar smoke, particularly around the pool room area, when smoking is not allowed, of course, in the building. Osgood was a perpetual cigar smoker. Other guests have reported being touched while sleeping, or of smelling the scent of fresh lilacs in mid-winter. Housekeepers report seeing people reflected in mirrors in empty rooms and of footprints on clean floors.

ACCESS

Take I-70 west to the Glenwood Springs exit #114. Take Highway 82 toward Aspen, and turn off at Carbondale onto 133 to Redstone. The castle is one aristocratic mile beyond the town of Redstone. Contact Redstone Castle for the hours of operation as they are in transition. Call 970-963-9656 or visit their website at www.red stonecastle.us (Note: the .us on the website is correct.)

THE CASTLES THAT WERE

The Castle at River Front

imagination then, and made me believe that the castle can be a bridge to connect us to a romantic past.

Research proved my castle not just one of imagination. The structure, originally known by the mundane name of "Castle of Commerce and Culture," was the cornerstone of Denver's first amusement park, River Front, and had indeed, *existed* in the romantic and storybook era of Victoria, around the 1880s. However, where the original park and castle once stood, we now can view the "heart transplant" of the century.

The new modern River Front Park springs up in the vitals of Denver on the same ground as the original park. An epitome of modern design, glass condos rise high amid designer patios, with fountains, sculpture, and futuristic bridges reaching out to allow and encourage access to the downtown. The angioplasty of the Highlands Pedestrian Bridge pumps new life into once-atrophic Platte Street and the Highlands area itself, which though very much alive these days, certainly welcomes this transfusion of traffic. Stunning Riverfront 2007 is a modern day phoenix rising from the ashes of the River Front Park of over one hundred and twenty years ago. Thus, the castle today leaves only a legacy of the name, River Front, wherein it was once the crown jewel.

HISTORY OF THE CASTLE

The castle was the creation of businessman John Brisben Walker, and was built of lava from Castle Rock, Colorado. It rose three stories tall, with solid rock battlements and a tower rising above truncated

THE CASTLE AS IT WAS

This is a "Once Upon a Time" story about a castle I remember seeing as a child, some sixty years ago, that just …disappeared. Perhaps it was the mystery in the memory of that castle beneath the Sixteenth Street overpass (then called a viaduct)—a strange location for a page out of a fairy tale book and rather like discovering a dragon in your nearby vacant lot—that ignited my

walls—as fort-like as any self-respecting castle. Walker built it as a showcase to prove to the world that his beloved Colorado led other states in agriculture, manufacturing, commerce, mining, and the arts. Fairs were held there, and the castle held a permanent exhibit of Colorado's products, as well as works of local artists. The art museum and mineral exhibit were two of its most popular attractions.

Buying two and three acres at a time, Walker had gathered forty acres of land along the Platte River, finishing the purchase in 1880 and creating the park itself between Wazee and Platte Streets. The castle was built one year later at the enormous cost of $80,000. Surrounding it were spacious lawns interspersed with multiple attractions to amuse the people of Denver whenever they had time for leisure. On Sundays in particular, gentlemen in cheviot suits and black bowlers would arrive via the cable car, their ladies gowned in bustled frocks and feathered hats. It was a popular trend to spend the day in Denver's first amusement park, a sanctuary of broad, green grounds with a movable grandstand seating five thousand people, where concerts with star attractions brought from New York were held on weekends. The Platte River had been dammed to make it deep enough to float a sidewheeler, which placidly paddled from Fifteenth to Nineteenth streets, with a band playing on deck. Historians relate that Gilbert and Sullivan's *H.M.S. Pinafore* was actually performed on a ship anchored in the river. A baseball diamond and a quarter-mile track were distributed among a myriad of gardens, trees, and benches, where the tightly corseted ladies, shaded by their parasols, could catch their collective breathes and enjoy the atmosphere. But of all the glories of the park, the castle was the capstone feature.

J. B. Walker never did anything on less than a grandiose scale. Besides the daily attractions, the Fourth of July fireworks were breathtakingly dramatic, and were usually held on a stage inside the great wooden postern gates of the castle under the stars. Spectators sat inside the bailey area and on the balcony lining the castle's great hall. One year the show included "The Burning of Rome," "The Last Days of Pompeii," and "The Fall of Sebastopol," holy cow—all in one evening. And interspersed in the intermissions were ballerinas, just to assure Walker that his audience wouldn't wander away. This castle then, was the

convention center of the 1880s, providing Denver with exhibit halls, one of its first museums, and a live theater in a regal setting. Walker was one of the most imaginative and resourceful pioneers in the West. Denver's first rodeo was also held at River Front, and later the first auto race, at a location nearby.

For the early years, Walker's park was a smashing success, but later the Elitch's Zoological Gardens and the Lakeside Amusement Park were built, and Denver's population could not support this much entertainment. Soon revenues were failing to pay for his lavish entertainment schedule. In 1889, Walker left for New York City to become a magazine publisher, and in 1894, he sold the park lands to the railway companies, which were now surrounding the park itself. Several years later the castle was put to use as a washroom by road crews, and as a laundry room for the Pullman Company.

By 1900, the castle was the only relic remaining of River Front Amusement Park. In the middle of a train yard, the grey stone of the building, daily dusted with coal smoke from belching locomotives, had turned to a near-black. In November, 1951, someone noticed smoke seeping from the boarded-up windows of the old castle, and sounded a fire alarm. Bales of hay had been stored there, and it's probable that the fire was caused by the ignition of gas fumes from the baled hay, causing a spontaneous combustion. With all doors and windows locked, it took several hours before the fire was discovered. Seven pieces of fire apparatus arrived at the building to find huge clouds of mushrooming smoke and the flames out of control. It was impossible for the firemen to gain entrance. Only minutes

The 1951 fire destroyed the castle.

later, the roof collapsed. Firemen later reported that when they arrived the walls of the stone building were so hot that "bits of rock were popping loose all over the place, like firecrackers."

For two hours, eleven fire hoses poured water on the building, and though no one was injured or killed, the $10,000 of hay was a total loss, as well as the stored files of the Rio Grande Railroad.

A sad ruin of scorched and collapsing stone lay in the rail yard only months before the remains of the castle were carted away to make way for more tracks.

JOHN BRISBEN WALKER

John Brisben Walker's biographical material can be found in the chapter on Falcon Castle, as that was the home he built for himself and for his family.

John Brisben Walker's name is not a familiar one to the people of Denver, or elsewhere in Colorado, and that hardly seems fair. We have no Walker Avenue or a building of that name. Nonetheless, many things we take for granted were his ideas in the first place. Today we can thank him for the foresight for fighting for the establishment of our mountain parks system. He predicted that Colorado would be a tourist haven and planned for that end, even though he was ridiculed by his peers in the Denver Chamber of Commerce. Such irony.

His River Front Park was a first of many things for Colorado: the first rodeo was held there, and it was the city's first amusement park. The castle was Denver's first museum, both of art and of commerce, and actually, our first shopping center. This man was prescient beyond belief.

His purchase of 40,000 acres in and around Morrison included what we now know as Red Rocks, and he was the first person to hold outdoor entertainment in this perfectly acoustical setting. He also foresaw Morrison as a tourist Mecca, which it never became. Nevertheless, he certainly had the right idea.

Ironically, he is known, if at all, for being the man who developed the magazine, *Cosmopolitan*, into a gigantic success. *Cosmopolitan*, until resurrected by Helen Gurley Brown, nearly passed, like the smoke from his vanished castles. Walker's dreams literally did go up in smoke, but what a luminary the man was.

The residents of Colorado owe many thanks to pioneers like John Brisben Walker. We can thank him for the Berkeley and Highlands areas of Denver, for Regis University, our mountain parks system, the name River Front, and more, I'm sure, that I've yet to learn.

CASTLES THAT WERE

Crystal Castle
(LEADVILLE'S ICE PALACE)

We speak of a castle as a manifestation of a person's dream, but this structure, a dream brought to reality by an entire town, was, quite literally, a "castle in the air." A gigantic, crenelated creation of ice, it perched at the apex of the highest incorporated city in North America, two-mile high Leadville, Colorado.

Leadville's "Crystal Castle," also called "Ice Palace," stood a syntillating, monstrous glow, up against the dark, chilled sky in the January, February, and March nights of 1896. It was the *raison d'être* for the joyous carnival that had sustained the high spirits of Leadvillites for much of the previous year. The huge castle, built entirely of clear blocks of ice over a wooden frame, covered five acres, with small turrets on each corner and the front and back entrances flanked by larger towers. The octagonal towers at the main entrance loomed ninety feet high and measured forty feet across. In front of the great arched entrance stood Lady Leadville, an ice sculpture nineteen feet high in addition to the twelve feet of her pedestal. Her arm extended to the right, pointing toward the mountains where Leadville miners had dug out $200 million worth of minerals in the year of 1894. Although this had been a record year, it was a swan song for the town, as the silver standard had collapsed the year before, and Leadville was facing hard times.

The buttressed outer walls of the castle stood thirty-eight feet high, surrounding an area 320 feet

A frozen exhibit

by 450 feet. At the back of the castle were the two south towers, a lesser sixty feet in height with thirty foot diameters. Like a true castle, the walls were crenelated in Norman style, with a twenty-foot passage way between the outer walls and the walls of the interior buildings. This passageway was roofed, allowing comfortable traffic flow for workmen and patrons.

Centrally located inside the castle was a large ice-skating rink, 90 feet wide by 180 feet long, which could accommodate one thousand skaters at a time. A wall, twenty feet high along three sides of the rink, was topped by ice pillars fifteen feet apart and joined at the top by arches of ice. Each pillar shone with embedded electric lights of many colors. From the wood trusses above the rink hung stalactites of ice.

A ballroom, fifty by eighty feet, adjoined the rink to the west, with a window between for mutual admiring. On the east side, the auxiliary ballroom was also used as a dining room, with the kitchen off to the back and a window looking onto the skating rink. The lounges, or reception rooms, were lavishly furnished with plush couches and throw-rugs, as well as ornate paintings on the walls.

The Palace of Living Art and Illusions was a theater with its own building, separated from the main structure of the castle by a walled-in passage, which was bisected by a porte cochere, a pass-through for horse-drawn coaches. The theater presented live shows as well as movies, all quite tastefully done with the exception of one notorious midnight venture when they offered a show where the former "goddesses and sea nymphs"

from previous shows were to be presented to the audience "as was"—no clothes. The theater was well filled, but with a police raid, the performance was cancelled and all were refunded their dollar.

Another auxiliary building was the Riding Gallery that was connected to the main area by a twenty-seven foot archway. It held a large carousel and was popular even after the carnival was over.

The features were extraordinary. Electric lights with colored bulbs were placed in and around the ice blocks so that the castle actually glowed at night. Of course, shows and entertainment ran from noon well into the evening hours. Exhibits from multiple companies—table delicacies of trout, fish, meat, veggies, and even pickles, were frozen in ice blocks, as well as clothing and medicines. Coors froze a beer display in a pyramid that was so large it took up the entire northwest tower, although alcohol sales were not allowed in the building. Ice sculptures, which had been carved in secrecy, were revealed upon the opening of the castle. Most of them were related to the mining industry, and were depictions of burros or miners, and were placed throughout the castle and in archways.

Two toboggan runs were built, the longer 1,200 feet, and the shorter, 900 feet. To begin, one climbed up a twenty-foot ramp, then aboard the toboggan, to fly down the steep ramp at a breathtaking pace. From there, the toboggan was routed down the street, finally slowing to a stop. Open until late in the evening, each course was lit by hanging arc lights of 2,000 candle power with colored globes set fifteen feet apart. The fares were a

nickel one way and a dime for round trip. (I assume the passengers got to sit on the toboggan while being pulled up the hill.) The first day alone, the toboggan run brought in $850, with 25 percent of the gross going to the Leadville Crystal Carnival Association, who had organized funding for the castle.

As a special exhibit, the Denver and Rio Grande Railroad built a gold-trimmed working model of a train engine, which cost an enormous $1,500, and was placed in the north-east corner.

Musicians were brought in to play for the many parades, and for the skating and dancing. Most notable was the Ft. Dodge Cowboy Band,

"Lady Leadville"

which performed from the first parade in November until the closing day in March. The twenty-member band was paid $100 a day, quite a haul then, and split up between the members.

A committee had chosen Tingley S. Wood as Director General, a highly respected and successful businessman in Leadville. He made it clear from the beginning that this was a project belonging to the Leadville community, and it was mandatory that each citizen dress in bright colors and costumes when working at or attending the castle events. The dowdy, depressed town responded enthusiastically, putting on its party clothes, painting, and fixing every store and home, with the homeowners sprucing up and doubling up the kids in hopes of housing a paying overnight guest or two.

No paved roads led to Leadville in 1896, but three railroads serviced the mining town: the Denver and Rio Grande came from the Pueblo area through Denver; the Colorado Midland from eastern Colorado; and the South Park from the western slope. The carnival surely was of benefit to them as well, as they re-routed their trains whenever they could. Special rates were given for large groups, and for the people in general, a car with a sleeping compartment cost $5 round trip, which included a ticket into the castle. To publicize the carnival, a group of costumed Leadvillites rode all over the state soliciting and advertising their carnival, resulting in much traffic from winter sports clubs of every sort, from snow skiing to curling. Their enthusiasm was contagious.

Special days were held for every imaginable group, with a Kids' Day, a Sunday School Day, Stockbrokers,' Wheelmen's, Daughters of the American Revolution, and even a day designated "Colored People's Day." A parade was held from the railway station to the castle, with the townspeople in costume, and the special guests exploiting their symbols, as did the Shriner's with their fezes and real camels.

HISTORY OF THE CASTLE

Leadville was founded in 1877 near the new silver deposits, setting off the Colorado Silver Boom, and by 1880, was one of the world's largest silver camps with a population of over 40,000. In 1893, the bottom fell out of the silver market. Many mines were closed up, and by 1895, the town was depleted to a population of 14,477. With most out of work, Leadvillites faced a winter in this two-mile high village that promised to be long, hard, and very cold. And perfect for an Ice Castle.

Ice palaces had been built before. Russia had started it all long ago in the 1700s. The cold and northern cities of Montreal and St. Paul had turned their drab winters into carnival time with castles of their own. Leadville, though much further south, had altitude. High, dry, and cold are the winters there, and in the lean summer of 1895, someone, perhaps Mr. Edwin Senior, came up with an inspiration—an ice castle and Crystal Carnival that would employ the townspeople and bring in crowds and revenue for the ailing village.

Mr. Senior had a major fault—he didn't drink. As first director of the Leadville Crystal Carnival, he certainly got the citizens behind him, but the prospective income was from the banks

Replica of the ice castle at the National Mining Museum in Leadville.

and bars, Leadville having eighty-three saloons at the time. By the end of September, Senior had only raised $4,000. Gracefully, he resigned and the committee was then headed by Tingley Wood, who apparently *did* drink. Whatever the reasons, the pot was quickly doubled. Wood proposed a deal to the committee. He would head the Crystal Carnival enterprise if they would promise to raise $20,000. Swallowing their respective Adam's apples, they agreed, and Wood was in. A wise businessman who headed several companies, one of Wood's first acts as Director General was to incorporate the enterprise as the Leadville Crystal Carnival Association.

St. Paul, Minnesota, had built ice castles for several years, and it was from this city that Wood hired architect C. E. Joy. A castle bigger and more glamorous than any ice castle built before, was what Leadville shouted for.

A large, undeveloped plot of land on the highest point in the city was leased for one dollar a year, and cleared of trees and brush. By November 16, 1895, 307,000 board-feet of lumber was delivered, and the framework was started. Wood figured that to finish by the holiday season, they would need to lay 200 tons of ice a day, and horse-drawn wagons began hauling huge blocks of ice from the Evergreen Lakes southwest of the city, the Twin Lakes, and the Arkansas River. Some blocks were as large as five feet by two feet by two, with a weight of up to six hundred pounds.

The cornerstone (cornercube?) was laid on November 25, and they were off and running— well, walking fast. The 250 to 350 men building the frame and laying ice created the entire structure in thirty-six days, despite the setback of several sabotaging warm Chinook winds. The blocks were hoisted on top of each other and hot water poured over them, freezing faster than cold water and creating an iron-hard wall. When the sun shone too warmly, the walls were protected with huge muslin sheets purchased out-of-pocket by Tingley Wood.

By now, $20,000 was just start-up money. Concessions were sold, and merchants fought to get a booth, selling food and candies, special medals struck for the Carnival, every gadget you'd find today at a large festival. The merchants were charged a fee for the booth plus a percentage of their take, and this sweetened the pot, as did further donations, and later the ticket sales. There was even a sale of stock, at one dollar a share. By December 24, the collection was $40,000, but the costs with labor and materials came to a minimum of $60,000. It is believed that Tingley Wood made up the deficit himself. Lighting had been added in December to allow night work, miserable as it was in the below-zero nights. On December 30, with an all-out effort, the ice masons laid a record 254 *tons* of ice in one day. And on December 31, the last load of ice was delivered.

Ice Palace skating rink

Although the castle was still not finished, New Years Day, 1896, was the first official parade and the opening of the toboggan runs. The parade was all-inclusive—even shops were closed so the employees could participate or watch. Led by the carnival officials, next came probably the most memorable sight, a small cart holding five-year-old Helen Marechal pulled by her two pug dogs. Half the town was parading and half cheering them on, with the loudest applause for the builders of the castle, who marched at the end as a group. On January 4, the castle opened to a substantial crowd—at least a thousand on the train from Denver—though work was still going on inside.

The official opening was on January 15, which was designated as Colorado Press Day. The north towers were finally finished and completely lit up. Rockets blazed in the sky and fireworks sprayed above the ecstatic crowd. Inside, the castle was jammed with merrymakers; one could hardly move, let alone skate, but the mood was ebullient. A lavish dinner was served at 11:30 P.M., so the festivities must have gone on well into the night.

A horse show was given on January 19, with a specially trained brigade of thirty horses using no bridles or harnesses. This was a major hit. Other days were dedicated to groups or to clubs, and every in-coming train was met with a parade that escorted the newcomers to the castle gate.

February found customers coming to the castle from all over the world. On March 7, a banquet was given by Wood to honor the exhibitors with medals and monetary gifts. And by now, the town was rather exhausted from its gargantuan effort.

The weather was warming up, business was slacking off, and with the driving forces running out of steam, it was clear that the end was in sight. March 28 was set as the closing date, and the party atmosphere hit high gear once more. Although the snow had been considerably below normal all winter, it fell in soft clumps as the entire town stood in front of the north towers, watching a glorious display of fireworks, courtesy of Tingley Wood, until the final fireburst. The castle was now officially closed.

AFTERWORD

The ice rink was used for skating until the first of June, when it just got too slushy. Much of the lumber was taken away by people who were building their own houses, and in early June, a major strike by the miners brought in the state militia, who used some of the boards to build their own housing.

The Leadville Ice Palace or Crystal Castle I believe is the largest creation of its kind the world has ever seen. It is the only one ever completely utilized, and surely, the only one ever built by an entire town. And though it physically disappeared, it really has never left.

HAUNTED

I do believe the Crystal Castle or Ice Palace itself still lives in Leadville. Permanent replications are in its museums, and the beautiful Ice Palace Inn, a B&B, is built on the same hill as the original with some of its lumber. Sadly, there may never be another as grand in scale and detail, but its memory certainly lingers on.

Cutthroat and Hovenweep Castles

THE CASTLES OF CUTTHROAT AND HOVENWEEP

In the introduction to this book, I spoke of some of the early castles or fortifications built, mostly in the European area. With this chapter, we have our own American version—the towers and stoneworks built by the Ancestral Puebloans in our Four Corners Area over seven hundred years ago. Hovenweep National Monument, one of the settlements of the Ancestral Puebloans (preferred term to Anasazi) in this area, is unique because the people here built towers dating from the mid- to late 1200s. Of the six clusters of Native American ruins at Hovenweep, four are in Colorado: Cutthroat Castle, Holly, Hackberry/Horseshoe, and Goodman Point, with two more in Utah.

Not castles you say? Castle qualifications are: *stone*, check; *towers*, check; *fortification*, check; *moat*, will a canyon do?; and *crenelation*,—well, bumpy on top. And also they have a Great House. These sound pretty castley to me. Besides our National Park tags them as castles, and who are we to argue with the Feds?

Hovenweep National Monument visitor center is reachable by paved road. There, the ranger station provides a requisite short film before you trek on foot some three hundred yards down a concrete path, which ends at a canyon and the first ruins. To reach Hovenweep Castle, turn right and follow the dirt and stone path atop Little Ruin Canyon about half a mile to the canyon's end. Here, I think, is the

Above and left: Cutthroat Castle

Hovenweep Castle

finest example of the expert engineering and masonry skills of these people. The Ancestral Puebloans adapted their construction designs to the uneven surfaces of rock slabs, so the buildings just seem to grow onto the rocks of the canyon as if they are appendages. Although the purpose of building the towers is controversial, it has been determined that parts of Hovenweep Castle define an apparent solar calendar. The building is aligned so that the light falls through small openings and illuminates a marker at sunset during the solstices of summer and winter. Also, note how small the openings are—some only mere slits and others too small for human entry. (Corroboration of their advanced knowledge of celestial activity is the structure of the Great House, which is aligned with

Ruins above Little Ruin Canyon

Square Tower

despite marginal growing conditions, these people raised corn, beans, squash, and other crops in small fields and terraces by diverting water from the streams to irrigate.

Square Tower, for which this group is named, sits down in the canyon right behind Hovenweep Castle, and was built on a rock surface. The Puebloans constructed more buildings here inside the canyon than can be seen today since they needed to entrap and defend the precious water that sustained the multitudes of people who once lived here. However, the structures built on solid sandstone, usually atop the canyon rim, have lasted seven hundred years, while those on the soft surface of the canyon bottom are in various states of condition, many now only rubble.

The trail continues around the canyon rim another mile and a half, giving the hiker a tour of the entire Square Tower Group. It's a good idea to remember bottled water and a head cover as there is no shade from the sun, and the white rock trail can make for a thirsty trip on a hot day.

Cutthroat Castle, located in Colorado and at the upper end of the National Monument complex, is unique because it is not located at the head of a canyon, but further downstream. The Cutthroat Group seems to have a large number of kivas or ceremonial structures—here, in relative abundance—and is somewhat isolated from the other five groups, only incorporated into the Hovenweep group in 1956. In fact it takes a nine-and-a-half-mile drive to the trailhead with an all-terrain vehicle and an additional mile and a half hike to reach it.

Chimney Rock, a structure of two natural pillars of stone, on a ridge located between Durango and Pagosa Springs. A mere twenty years ago, scientists determined that this Great House is a precisely aligned lunar observatory.)

Holding lit grass torches from the tower tops, modern researchers discovered a line-of-sight network from tower to tower—the Hovenweep telephone. Other indications of a well developed society can be seen here in the outlines of multiple-room pueblos, rubble from towers that have collapsed, rock art, even jewelry, pottery, and clothing. And

In Ancestral Puebloan religion, the kiva functions much as our churches do, connecting the inhabitant to another world. Most kivas are round structures dug into the ground, which connect the inhabitant to the world below. The entrance, however, is through the roof, which is related to the world above. The kiva was also a home for the Puebloans, as their lives were intertwined with their religion. With the kiva as the central area, auxiliary rectangular rooms were built around it for sleeping or storage. Cutthroat Castle itself is an anomaly as its kiva rests on top of a boulder. This kiva is surrounded by another room that is entered from below, through a separation in the boulder.

Although the Hovenweep area seems totally isolated now, it was actually part of a vast network of prehistoric villages, remarkably advanced in the development of agricultural abilities and covering a large area where the four states come together.

HISTORY OF HOVENWEEP

Although there is evidence of human habitation in this area for thousands of years, it was in the mid-1800s that the first Europeans came upon the deserted ruins. The name "Hovenweep," Paiute/Ute for "deserted valley," was adapted by pioneer photographer William Henry Jackson in 1874, and quite accurately describes the desolation of these canyons and mesas wherein the ancient farmers cultivated and irrigated their crops. Though we know the natives in this Four Corners area as Anasazi, they are more accurately called Ancestral Puebloans, and the fascinating thing about them, besides their mysterious exodus, is the variation in the composition of their living areas. While the better known Mesa Verde tribe built into the cliffs, the Hovenweep people, also members of the Mesa Verde tribe, had a penchant for building towers and massive castle-like buildings with shapes that varied, including square, rectangle, round, D-shaped and horseshoe.

The Hovenweep area began with small, scattered units—pueblos built on the mesa around 1100—and evolved after 1200 into sophisticated masonry-walled pueblos, with large structures interspersed, often at the head of the canyons. Water was the life blood of the Ancestral Puebloans, which, in this dry, arid climate, they diverted into the fields to grow food, using innovative farming methods like terrace farming and irrigation. Modern scientists examined tree rings from the logs used for construction in the area and found that from 1250 to 1300 there was a severe

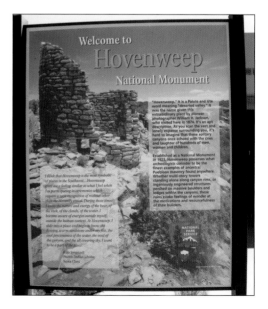

Hovenweep Castle

drought, which likely caused a large migration of the Puebloan people. Additionally, there now are no trees here, although logs were a corporate part of the construction. This indicates a depletion of a vital building material and fuel. Not everyone left however, as they are believed to be the ancestors of the modern tribes of the Hopi, Zuni, and Pueblo.

Hovenweep is an amazing trip into the past, particularly because the surroundings are as they were seven hundred years ago. For those interested in the unique Anasazi/Puebloan sites, other interesting venues and alternative styles of living can be seen in nearby Mesa Verde or as far away as Chaco Canyon in New Mexico.

ACCESS

To reach Hovenweep National Monument, drive to Cortez, Colorado, in the southwest corner of our state. From there, take Highway 160 east for seven miles to the sign indicating a road on the right leading to Hovenweep. This road leads through a variety of landscapes for forty-two miles until the area becomes desert-like and empty, except for scrub bush. By following signs, the road leads to a very good ranger station with a trail leading to Little Ruin Canyon and the towers. Also, we are now in, woops, Utah, but that's rather splitting hairs, since there's no state line in sight.

NOTE: While the Ancestral Puebloan ruins in the Square Tower group can be reached by foot, the outlying sites are on dirt roads that are impassable when wet and only suitable for high-clearance vehicles when dry.

CASTLES THAT WERE

Falcon Castle

THE CASTLE TODAY

Currently, at the top of Mount Falcon you'll find a beautiful mountain park with a view, but this was certainly not all that John Brisben Walker had in mind for his legacy. Where a grand castle once stood, and close by the foundation of what he hoped would be the presidential Summer White House—now stand only piles of stones atop a public mountain park. Walker's dream did literally turn to dust, but his ideas and foresight live on.

To reach the skeletal remains of Walker's dream, it's necessary to hike or drive up Mount Falcon, right above Morrison, Colorado, and walk several miles. Trails lead to a pinnacle overlooking the 4,000 acres, once owned by Walker, and now belonging to the people of Colorado. Up top, the staunch stones of the walls and several fireplaces survive to either remind us, or to provoke inquiry into, the Colorado pioneer who, among other things, certainly initiated the preservation of land along the Front Range of our Rockies.

Fittingly, it takes a healthy walk through Jefferson County's Open Space to reach the ruins. Coming in from the top of Mount Falcon via Parmalee Gulch, it's easy to follow the signs to the Mount Falcon parking lot, and on foot, take Castle Trail east. About a quarter mile along the path, you can look to the left and see the ruins silhouetted against the skyline to the north, with the main chimney the distinguishing feature. It's another half mile to reach the site.

Main fireplace

Falcon's Nest, photo taken after the fire

Up close, the castle ruins look more like a piece of folk art than the remains of a luxury home. The one-story walls stand alone, except for the single tall finger of the chimney. Like a jigsaw puzzle, the pink granite rocks are of various sizes and shapes, fitting snuggly together. Custodial Jefferson County has fenced off the delicate ruins and reinforced the walls, sometimes by slathering them with exterior mortar, giving the area a rather haphazard appearance. But this is belied by the severe symmetry of the squared walls and the interesting shapes of some of the window openings. It's difficult to imagine grand living here, as all that's left rises among wild grass and bare

ground, reminding me somewhat of cattle pens. Yet photos show us that it once was a gracious home of elegant woodwork and bay windows of cut glass, expensively furnished with works of art and the best of everything available.

The building site itself must cover a quarter of an acre. In a "U" shape with a west and east wing, it surrounds a sheltered terrace area, where elegant meals were served and parties were once held. The north area or bottom of the "U" overlooks a great vista with a view of Mount Morrison and Bear Creek Canyon. The Walkers lived here on the very top of the world at a time when John Brisben Walker was literally King of the Hill, and one of the most important and foresighted men in the blossoming city of Denver, pushing hard for Colorado to develop a system of mountain parks.

HISTORY OF THE CASTLE

John Brisben Walker had previously been an entrepreneur in Denver and the Colorado area. He left Denver in 1889 to go back East to Tarrytown, New York, and purchase the failing magazine, *Cosmopolitan*. He and his wife, Emily, divorced that same year.

In 1906, after selling his magazine publication at a tremendous profit, Walker returned to Colorado with a pocket full of money, a new wife Ethel, and four more children. He could well afford now to purchase 4,000 acres in and around Morrison and to create his own home atop Mount Falcon, a location with a view for 200 miles in any direction he wanted to look. The purchase included not only Mount Falcon and Mount Morrison, but a gigantic natural wonder of red sandstone locally known as the "Garden of the Angels," presently our Red Rocks Park. Part of the town of Morrison was also included in the sale.

Creation of the castle began in 1909. During construction, the Walker family lived in Morrison in a converted hotel, once called "Swiss Cottage," which had been previously used by the Jesuits as a college. Walker donated forty acres of his Berkeley Farm to the Jesuits, where they then created and developed a very proper college they named Regis.

Native granite was used for the Mount Falcon home's construction, and it was built at the apex of the mountain with views from Denver to Mount Evans. This was his "Falcon's Nest," a home with twenty-two rooms and eight fireplaces where he lived when he was in Colorado.

Although it was his dream come true, and though his life seemed ideal, it was a relatively short period of five years that Walker lived atop Mount Falcon. In 1916, Ethel died quite suddenly, and only two years later, the Walker home was destroyed, purportedly because of a lightning strike and resulting fire. Even though he moved into Denver, Walker never could give up his dream of building a Summer White House, though support for it waned year by year.

By 1926, Walker was nearly eighty years old and had run out of funds. According to the records, he lost the Mount Falcon property at a sheriff's sale resulting from a failure to record a deed. The property was then bought by the Kirchhof family, who later sold it to Jefferson County Open Space. This, ironically, resulted in a preservation of the area and created another mountain park. J. B. Walker would be pleased.

JOHN BRISBEN WALKER

He must have been a beautiful baby, since he sure was a handsome dude. Born in 1847 in his parents' country home on the Monogahela River near Pittsburgh, John Brisben Walker showed fire and enterprise from the get-go, and very early on was jumping from

163

one opportunity to the next, an Eliza crossing the ice floes.

As a youth, he first attended Gonzago College and later Georgetown University in Washington, D. C. Leaving Georgetown to accept an appointment to the U. S. Military Academy at West Point, he later resigned from The Point to go to China to serve as an advisor during China's change of their military system, and was eventually appointed a general. Returning to the United States in 1870, he was involved in the steel and iron production business for three years, and also ran as a Republican for Congress, but lost the election. By the age of twenty-six, he'd made and lost a fortune in West Virginia. Additionally, he'd married Emily Strother, "the prettiest girl in the valley of the Virginia." What a résumé.

By the time he was thirty, he had written articles on the mineral industry for the *Cincinnati Commercial Gazette*, and had been managing edi-

tor of *The Pittsburgh Telegraph* and later the Washington D.C. *Daily Chronicle*—work that would pay off handsomely later in his life.

Walker must have run in the right circles. In 1879, the U. S. Secretary of Agriculture asked him to go out West and investigate the viability of growing alfalfa in a dry, thin-air climate, and it was this venture that introduced him to Colorado. Buying 1,600 acres for a total of $1,000 north of Denver, he created "Berkeley Farm," and successfully produced alfalfa as a cash crop. Concurrently, he bought up acreage along the Platte River. The year after, in 1880, he began the creation of River Front Amusement Park (see the Castle at River Front). Meanwhile, he and his wife Emily were living in a north Denver area that he, in honor of his Scotch-Irish ancestry, called "The Highlands." They raised their eight children in a home at 3520 Newton Street, though he wasn't there much as he traveled extensively. Walker was very active in the Denver community and was a member of the Chamber of Commerce for many years.

There obviously must have been trouble in paradise. Some time during the late 1880s, Emily filed for divorce from John and it was granted.

In 1889, Walker moved back East to Tarry-town, New York, where he purchased the faltering *Cosmopolitan* magazine. Certainly, the develop-ment of the magazine became his greatest finan-cial achievement. Walker spiced up the magazine with articles appealing to just about every walk of life. In addition to poetry and fiction, there were stories on Persia, the West Indies, Sweden, and Guatemala; articles on beauty, fashion, club life, and suffrage. Famous writers such as Mark Twain, Robert Lewis Stevenson, and H. G. Wells pub-lished their fiction in the magazine. Stephen Crane, author of *Red Badge of Courage*, was first

introduced to the world through *Cosmopolitan* magazine. Walker was a pioneer in writing pieces aimed at a female audience. With such eclectic material his audience ballooned, and under his tutelage his magazine rose from a puny circulation of 10,000 to an eventual world-wide audience of some 400,000.

His River Front Amusement Park had thrived for the first several years, but perhaps because of the collapse of silver as a commodity and the following recession, business had fallen off until, by 1893, J. B. could no longer pay for the lavish entertainment for which his park was famous. That particular year was a fulcrum for many a Denver speculator, and I'm sure it was no asset that the owner and creator of the park often traveled half a continent away. In 1894 Walker sold the now-faltering River Front Park to the encroaching railroads. The castle there was then demoted to washroom and

laundry, and later used by the Denver Women's Club to distribute food to poor children.

In 1895 J. B. bought the patent to the Stanley Steamer and became president of the Stanley Automobile Company of America. First he bought an old building that he renovated to become a factory for manufacturing Locomobile steam cars in Philips Manor, New York. He then built his own factory outside of New York. This enterprise eventually ended up losing money in contrast to the success of the magazine, as J. B. was betting on steam to outlast and outsell the combustion engine. Ford won, Walker lost, in this instance. But the joy of driving the Stanley Steamer certainly balanced his disappointment. Many a Stanley Steamer later chugged up the road on Mount Falcon. In fact, in a large meadow at the top, many a gentlemanly contest of speed was held. Interestingly, Walker also was sponsor of the first American auto race in 1907.

As the saying goes, Walker was frequently galloping off simultaneously in many directions at once—a trademark, it seems, of a person with a very active brain. Often called quixotic, he was reported to pull men off of one job to work on another of his projects, which is perhaps how he could run two huge corporations at the same time, as he did the aforementioned two. This seemed to be a life-long trait.

In 1905, Walker sold his very successful *Cosmopolitan* magazine to William Randolph Hearst for a million dollars, according to many reports. He then returned to Denver with his new wife, Ethel Richmond Walker, and their four children.

Atop Mount Falcon, Walker built his new home with solid stone and eight fireplaces and a view 200 miles in every direction. From Morrison, he built a funicular railway straight to the top of Mount Morrison, with a tea house at the pinnacle. He also built hiking trails and an observation deck. Directly to the north of his mountain, a portion of his land purchase included a strange opening between two towering red sandstone rock formations, which Walker foresaw as a wonderful outdoor theater. He renamed this area "Garden of the Titans," and by doing so defied a curse laid by a Judge Luther on anyone who might change the name from Garden of the Angels. In 1910, the first outdoor concerts were held in what we now know as Red Rocks Amphitheater. The following year, star soprano of the Metropolitan Opera, Mary Garden, sang there and was enthralled. "Never in any opera house in the world over have I found more perfect acoustic properties … I predict that someday twenty thousand people will assemble there to listen to the world's greatest masterpieces." From the beginning, the "Garden of the Titans" was a huge success.

Walker was ahead of his time in wanting to conserve open space for the people of Colorado, and to promote tourism. In 1912, as member of the Denver Chamber of Commerce, he loaded his peers into a caravan of Stanley Steamers and drove them on his zig-zag road to a prepared luncheon atop his mountain. Whether because of the food or the view, they were convinced, and very much agreed with the idea of open space for the populace. Now with positive endorsement, the people of Denver passed a charter amendment to allow a mill levy for the purchase of mountain parks. This was the spark igniting the city to create many parks in the foothills area, beginning with Genesee in 1913, and followed by many more land conservancies that we have today.

In 1911 J. B. proposed the Summer White House, adjacent to his own castle on Mount Falcon, as a summer retreat for the president of the United States (see Summer White House chapter). But with castles, Walker seemed to have a black thumb.

Maybe it was because he defied the curse, who can say? But Walker's luck took a nosedive. His plans for a grand castle as a Summer White House quite literally never got off the ground. The family lived in their glorious castle a mere four years before his beautiful wife, Ethel, died very suddenly, leaving her young children. As was her wish, she was buried somewhere on the property, although the location is not known. Walker did not want curiosity seekers to be gawking at the grave. Apparently Walker and the children moved out the next year, as the castle was vacant in 1918, when it was completely destroyed by what was officially designated as a lightning strike. Arson, though not proven, was another possibility, as the destruction was total.

Still, there were intermittent victories. In 1912, with the Denver Chamber's, and later Mayor Speer's backing, his dream of open spaces was begun with public approval and support. In 1915 Walker was invited by the Panama-Pacific Exposition in San Francisco to be the "Director of Exploitation," which he accepted, taking his family to California for quite awhile.

By 1926, Walker had run out of funds and moved back East. It is reported that he lost his acreage at a sheriff's sale from a failure to record a deed, and in 1928 the Garden of the Titans was bought by the City of Denver for pennies on the dollar, and renamed Red Rocks. Walker died dead broke in Brooklyn in 1931 at the age of 83.

SCANDAL

Why would a mother of eight children, married to a successful business man, divorce him? Emily Walker lived in a beautiful home and seemed to have an ideal life, but even in an age when divorce was a stigma, she divorced her locally famous husband. This was at the end of the 1880s, just about the time J. B. Walker left for the East Coast. Then a scant six years later, he returned with an entourage of a new wife and four children.

Is it possible that this very financially successful man was fathering two families at once? Emily stayed in the Denver area until her death in 1935, and it is reported that the children of the second marriage never cared to discuss the details of the situation.

As a side note, J. B. and Emily's son, John Jr., was sued for divorce in 1901 after six years of marriage. His wife had discovered him living with another woman as her husband.

ACCESS

The lower trails, used frequently by bikers who like a challenge, begin on the road between Morrison and Hwy 285 and are clearly marked. An easier access is by taking the Parmalee Gulch Road two and a half miles to Picutis Road and following signs up to Mount Falcon where there are two large parking lots and picnic areas.

CASTLES THAT WERE

Kittredge Castle

English-style medieval castle on the plains of Colorado in 1890, only two years after the completion of the Richthofen manor. Of Romanesque revival architecture, Kittredge's structure had massive stone arches, oriel windows, towers, of course, and a crenelated turret. A most imposing feature of the exterior was the great stone arch of the porte cochere under which guests drove their carriages to the front door. From there, they were escorted through more great arches to the portico, or large porch, and then to the huge, arched front door. Arches seemed to be the theme throughout the castle, with even the upper windows shaped like half circles. The stable also was a great stone building, matching the castle in design.

It is reported that Kittredge spent $80,000 in the construction, and an equal amount in furnishing it with rich oriental rugs, tapestries, chandeliers, and intricate woodwork. The lower floors were the living areas. On the first level, a great hall, or spacious living room, the art gallery, library, music room, and conservatory were all finished in heavy white oak trim with floors of white maple. The second level was all large bedrooms and baths. The most famous and peculiar feature of the home was that the third level held the kitchen and huge dining area, with seating for one hundred guests, and even a room for dancing. The home had no elevator, so any friend coming for dinner could work up an appetite climbing the winding stairs. Actually, Kittredge found the odor of cooking obnoxious and the confusion of culinary activity disquieting, so he had separated this area from the rest of the home. However, a solid wall of arched windows rewarded the visitors with fabulous views,

THE CASTLE AS IT WAS

"Anything you can do, I can do better." It may have been the stimulus of the Richthoften home that inspired Charles M. Kittredge to build a castle himself in the Montclair area in the late 1800s. Or perhaps there was something about all that open space that provoked the building of castles. Whatever the motivation, there arose an

with mountains to the west and the Great Plains eastward, so I imagine complaints were few. The kitchen was equipped with a dumb waiter, so snacks or even dinners could be delivered down to the lower levels, should that be appropriate.

HISTORY OF THE CASTLE

Built in 1890, the castle, with its grand dining room, was very apparently focused on entertaining. Being a strong family man, and motivated much as Richthofen had been, Kittredge's primary motive, most probably, was to build the castle for his wife, Sadie, and their two children, Claire and Charles, Jr. Sadly, a bare three years after moving into the castle, Sadie died. Kittredge, now a widower, and suffering from Denver's economic plunge, sold the castle to John H. Nichols, who shortly thereafter, sold it again to Mrs. Eddy Smith, who lived in the home until 1906.

Colonel W. E. Hughes, a wealthy rancher turned banker, next purchased the castle in 1906. Hughes had come with his family to Colorado in the early 1900s, where he started the Continental Trust Company. Already a successful businessman with large ranches in Texas and Colorado, Hughes was one of the leading stockmen in the state. Hughes substantially renovated the stable area and additional quarters to accommodate his many show horses and a bevy of servants.

William Edgar Hughes had been born in 1840 to a farm family in Illinois, and was of Scotch-Irish heritage, with the distinction of belonging to the Highland clan of Sir Walter Scott. While on his way to Colorado, he found himself stranded in Kansas City, and so spent three months herding sheep to Texas while he studied his law books. With the start of the Civil War, he joined the Texas Cavalry, and rose to become a colonel, returning after the war to sheep herding and studying, until he passed the bar exam. In 1867, he married Annie Peate, and when their only child, Eliza, was five, he packed up his family and moved to Dallas. There he founded the largest bank in the city, the City National Bank, making his fortune much as Kittredge had. Concurrently, Hughes was acquiring large ranches in Texas and Colorado, and also gaining a name as a financier and philanthropist.

Daughter Eliza married John W. Springer (see Springer Castle) and the couple had come to Denver in 1897, most likely for the climate, as she was

tubercular. Eliza died in 1904 before the age of forty, leaving her own young daughter, Annie. Colonel Hughes and his wife raised Annie in the castle until she married and became the wife of Lafayette Hughes, son of a senator. (Although the name is the same, they were no relation.) In memory of his daughter, Colonel Hughes loaned the castle to the Methodist church, which converted it to the Clifton-Hughes Training School for Girls. By 1910, the school was boarding girls between the ages of twelve and eighteen from broken homes, providing academic schooling, as well as music and religious training.

Around 1933, Annie became the sole heir to the castle after the death of her grandparents and deeded the building to The Children's Aid Society, which merged with the previous training school, and turned the castle into a home for teenage girls. Five years later, it was renamed Holland Hall after their executive director, Mary Holland. As an interesting aside, in the early 1950s, Hollywood used the Hall as a set in the movie, *The Glenn Miller Story*, with several of the Montclair children playing bit parts.

Later in the 1950s, the castle and grounds were sold to the Catholic Archdiocese. The entire place—castle, trees, even the spectacular lilac garden—was leveled in order to build a Catholic high school. And sadder yet, should you drive by Eighth and Oneida streets now, what remains is a grassy lot—not a school in sight. Perhaps some solace can be found in that the name of the park is "Kittredge."

CHARLES M. KITTREDGE

Charles Marble Kittredge was a descendent of English nobility, and a successful banker and real estate developer in Denver when he built his English castle-style home. Born in Ohio in 1857 into an upper middle-class family, one story reports that he was a drummer boy with the Wisconsin Regiment in the Civil War at age seven. Kittredge passed up a Harvard education to work in bridge building and construction, much like his well-known father, Cornelius. Coming to Denver in 1884, he first established a successful bank, which he sold for a comfortable profit. He then went into commercial real estate, building much of downtown Denver. An early project was the Kittredge

Building, built in 1891 and still located at Sixteenth and Glenarm streets. He had originally planned it as a two-story structure, until his father, Cornelius Van Ness Kittredge, arrived in town. Cornelius was himself a builder of bridges and had built America's first cantilever bridge at Niagara Falls and bridges for the Nickle Plate Railroad.

"What, two stories?" he berated. "No son of mine can so belittle the name of Kittredge, nor this queen city." At an outrageous cost of nearly $450,000, the building went up, *seven* stories, which made the Kittredge Building a monument—and the tallest structure in Denver. Unfortunately, the West was working up to the financial crisis of 1893 when the bottom fell out of the silver market, which comprised much of Denver's economic base. Both Kittredges were heavily invested in this enterprise, and Charles had just built his castle as well. The holder of a second mortgage on the downtown building filed to foreclose. Luckily, the actual day before the foreclosure, Charles Kittredge managed a loan to rescue the financially embarrassed builders, but it nearly ruined the reputations of the two men, and Charles Kittredge walked out of the loan office having mortgaged everything he owned. It was at this time too, that his wife Sadie died from a heart attack. The Kittredge Building seemed to be a very expensive enterprise indeed.

However, the building proved to be a true monument. Its design incorporated steel beams, iron columns and a granite and rhyolite façade, making it both attractive and durable. By far the tallest building in Denver, it had such innovations as electricity, steam heat, fireproofing, and eleva-

tors, and was perhaps the first true office complex in town. Early tenants were a mixture of physicians, architects, insurance agents, and attorneys. It had a rooftop beer garden and amusement park, with seating for over three hundred people. Five years later, it became the YMCA headquarters, where Denver's first baseball games were held under the direction of Dr. James Naismith, who was the alleged inventor of the sport.

The Kittredges, father and son, did recover from the bad years and built much of the downtown area of Denver. Their namesake building, Denver's first skyscraper, still stands at the corner of Sixteenth and Glenarm streets, housing Marlowe's, an upscale restaurant.

After the death of Sadie in 1894, Kittredge lived as a widower for seven years and then remarried. Anna von Myrbach came from German nobility and bore him two more children, daughter, Alma, and son, Cornelius. The Kittredge family now lived in an area of Denver called Montclair, in a home designed by the famous architect, William Lang. Charles Kittredge was helping develop this new area as well as an adjoining area known as Park Hill.

Foresighted and also an ardent lover of nature and the mountains, Kittredge anticipated tourism in Colorado and purchased some 40,000 acres up Bear Creek Canyon where he built a resort town, which he named after himself. He laid out the town and provided systems for delivery of water and electricity. Schools were set up for the children, and Charles himself acted as postmaster. He lived there from 1920 until he died in 1939 at the age of eighty-two, spending much of his time at his favorite hobby, writing poetry and prose.

ACCESS

You can reach Kittredge, Colorado, by traveling several miles from Morrison up Bear Creek Canyon toward Evergreen.

CASTLES THAT WERE

Summer
White House

THE CASTLE AS IT MIGHT HAVE BEEN

Perhaps a view with a vista of 200 miles stimulates ideas. In 1910, John Brisben Walker's new home, the Falcon's Nest, was nearing completion at the top of Mount Falcon when he came up with another grand plan. What better way to promote his beloved state of Colorado than to build another castle here at the top of the world for the president of the United States? With the tribulations of diplomacy, law making, and often difficult problem solving, the president could do no better than a superb summer get-away—a home, elegant but secluded, catching the first rays of the morning sun. To the west would be the serene, eternal and often snow-capped peaks, and to the east, the endless plains. With the world at your feet, who could not feel refreshed and ready to take on world problems?

Walker's plan called for "a veritable palace of the most original and picturesque design, the likes of which does not exist in this country. It will take rank with the existing palaces of European monarchs." Putting his money where his mouth was, he hired a company to pave a road up the mountain, as step

number one. Next, he ordered a cornerstone of Colorado Yule marble (the same marble used for the Lincoln Memorial) to be inscribed, "A gift to the President of the United States from the People of Colorado." President Taft was told of the plan and stated that nowhere could a better location be found.

By 1911, Walker had the ball rolling. The Denver Civic and Commercial Association jumped on board with their endorsement. J. A. Thatcher of the Denver National Bank kicked off subscription with a check for $500, and several other businesses contributed with donations toward reaching the initial cost estimate of $35,000.

Architect Jacques B. Benedict offered, free of charge, to design a four-towered castle with twenty-two rooms, constructed of Colorado granite. Benedict had arrived in Denver only two year's prior, and the castle, as flamboyant as he was, would certainly make him a household word. His plans show a cathedral-like area to the east, with towers rising above, and a terrace overlooking a drop of 1,500 feet into Bear Creek Canyon. The powers of the world would meet here, and surely find harmony, as the smallness and fragility of humankind had to be felt in this grand perspective. The Denver Dry Goods store volunteered to furnish its drawing room, while Daniels and Fisher would furnish the dining room. "The entire state is to be extended the privilege of assisting the project," stated *The Denver Post*, and predicted that the initial $35,000 necessary would be attained within the next thirty days.

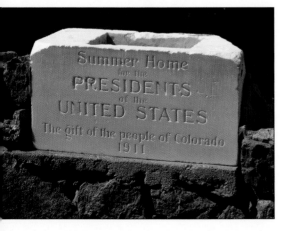

Architectural drawings by Benedict

With much ceremony, Walker broke ground for the castle in August of 1911, extolling the cool, dry climate of Colorado, comparing it to the miserable humid summers of Washington, D.C. The project was to belong to, and be financed by, the people of Colorado, as stated on the marble cornerstone. But the public stalled.

Walker went to the Denver merchants, now hoping to raise a public subscription, but got little response. Even the city council couldn't pass a resolution for collected donation. Undaunted, Walker asked each school child in the United States to contribute one dime, and some did. In order to inspire public interest, Walker put the engraved cornerstone on display at the corner of Stout and Seventeenth streets.

By 1912, it seemed that the project was in limbo, and the estimated cost had risen to $50,000

for the castle without its accoutrements. Walker suggested naming the rooms after Colorado cities—Denver, Leadville, Pueblo, Grand Junction, etc.—with hopes that each city would contribute to its own creation. Next, he proffered an exchange, promising to perform five public works in exchange for the support of his project, and all focused around his Red Rocks Park. He would first carve a replica of an Egyptian Sphinx in one of his huge red rocks, exact in size and detail. His second act would be to reproduce ten great prehistoric animals in cement, ranging in length from thirty to 104 feet, choosing animals whose fossils had been found in the area. For the third donation, he would produce a facsimile of a portion of the Mesa Verde cliff dwellings. The fourth and fifth contributions would increase and improve his natural

amphitheater for the comfort of his patrons. On the part of Denver, they were asked to improve the road to the summit of Mount Falcon and provide the funds for the structure. This, it was thought, would pay for the castle itself, and they could later add embellishments, which were estimated at $250,000.

By 1914, no real progress had been made. President Wilson was scheduled to be in Denver, and it was announced that he would lay the cornerstone. By this time, the United States was preparing to go to war, and although Wilson did come to Colorado, he did not lay the cornerstone. In July, Walker, with his entourage and a great deal of ceremony, hauled the stone up Mount Falcon and set it in place. This snub is something of a mystery, but Wilson was no fan of Walker, who was an ardent and very vocal pacifist.

In 1919, with the war at an end, Walker again approached the business community for funds. Again, the plan was touted in the newspapers as a viable one, but Walker and the press seemed to be the only proponents. The cornerstone, which for the past several years had been located in Morrison, was finally put in place by an entourage of businessmen. At its inception, the project had been page-one news, but by 1926 it had been relegated to a small column on page fourteen. In the years in between, Walker's life had been devastated by several tragic events: his beloved wife had died suddenly in 1916, and his home, the Falcon's Nest was struck by lightning in 1918, resulting in almost total destruction. By now, Walker himself was in his seventies.

Walker's final attempt to finance his dream castle was in 1927, when he tried to sell construction bonds for $1,000 each. Anyone contributing this amount, he proposed, could use the Summer White House when the president wasn't there. It was rather like the first time-share. He also offered his Garden of the Titans to Denver for a bargain price. It was too little, too late. By now, financially strapped himself, his properties were lost to foreclosure, and Denver picked up the Red Rocks Park for a mere $54,000.

John Brisben Walker was an amazing and foresighted dreamer, but perhaps this greatest of all dreams was just not meant to be. In hindsight, an old or older man, as the president often is, could not comfortably move from the White House at sea level to an elevation of almost 8,000 feet, and func-

tion at top level for his summer month in Colorado. But the incredible persistence, foresight, and dedication of Walker give insight into a pioneer of Denver, and reflect on how he succeeded in other ventures, as he did with the magazine, *Cosmopolitan*.

J.J.B. BENEDICT

More information on John Brisben Walker can be found in the chapters on Falcon Castle and the Castle at River Front.

Jules Jacques Benois Benedict was the donor architect for J. B. Walker's dream of a Summer White House, and it is Benedict's plan, along with a low stone wall embedded with a marble cornerstone, that survive as remnants of that dream.

Benedict is remembered not only for his architecture, but also for his very quirky and individualistic nature, some of it commendable and some rather deplorable. Known as Jacques ("Jock"), or J. B., he was born in Chicago in 1879, the child of apparently well-off Austrian immigrants. As a youth, he and his mother spent much of the time in Europe, giving him an eclectic education and a bend toward the romantic architecture of the Old Country. Returning to the United States, he attended Massachusetts Institute of Technology; then later, he went back to Paris and the exclusive École des Beaux Arts. These influences are evident in almost everything he built.

Benedict returned to the United States and worked in Chicago and New York before coming to Denver, where he married into Denver society. As a personality, he wielded a double-edged sword—witty, clever, and a very popular dinner table guest. But this wit could have a cutting edge bordering on cruelty, sometimes commenting on others' failings. His wife's weight problem came up more than once. It may be that being an indulged child created a persona that was very self-assured, to the point of being cocky, and tinged with snobbishness. However, the talent and creativeness was certainly there, as Benedict's works provide a multitude of proof.

Professionally, J. B. was a perfectionist, often to the distress of the group who had hired him. He demanded full authority over each project, and was constantly on hand to inspect a work's progress, and scrutinizing every detail. Known for wearing spats and carrying a cane, he was famous for smashing unsatisfactory work, and many a plan was burned in a fit of temper.

On the other side of the coin, Benedict frequently donated his own money, time, or art objects to finish a work to his own satisfaction. In 1917, he personally raised an additional $4,000 for the Woodbury Library on Federal Boulevard when he felt the allotted $14,000 "would not let it be built well." He built and donated a children's wading pool in Cheesman Park, and lowered his fee to Littleton when building their city hall. In this respect, he was a true artist, putting the perfection of his creation before the money. His designs were often Italian Renaissance and reflected a definite European influence. Although popular as a society architect, he shunned the American

Institute of Architects and was blackballed from the Cactus Club, an exclusive men's organization, by two of his fellow craftsmen, who apparently couldn't abide his demeanor. He was similarly shunned from the "alliance" of architects who designed Denver's city and county building. He proffered his own design that was cast aside, but only after a decade of battle with Benedict and *The Denver Post* on one side, and the A.I.A., *Rocky Mountain News,* and Mayor Stapleton on the other. The public, however, loved his unique designs, and his works can be seen throughout the city.

After coming to Denver in 1909, Benedict's first important structure was the Church of Divine Science. By 1911, with his well-publicized design for the Summer White House, he became a household word and, despite being an outsider in the architectural world, was in great demand. He married into society in 1912, and his bride purchased 90 acres from a ranch in Littleton, which he turned into a country estate. Benedict remodeled his farm house, adding what his biographer, A. Reynolds Morse, called "an ornate and incongruous medieval wing." The estate was now called Wyldemere Farm, and the couple landscaped it with gardens, pools, and terraces. Littleton embraced him, and three of the town's most distinctive buildings are his design. The first was the city hall, now called the Town Hall Arts Center, built in 1920, and is an excellent example of his favorite Italian Renaissance style with graceful arches and ornamental detail. The second was the Carnegie Library, finished in 1927, and is now an upscale restaurant. In 1929, he rendered the Presbyterian Church on Main Street, an excellent example of his design for the practical.

Benedict designed Denver's Flatiron building in 1923, at 1669 Broadway, and made his own offices there until 1942, when he retired. A portfolio of his local works, created in 1925, includes many libraries and churches, as well as dozens of homes. He was prolific in designing mountain homes, using both native timber and stone to harmonize them with their surroundings. In fact, it is likely that the lure of the mountains probably brought Benedict to Colorado. Anne Waring Maer, who grew up in two of Benedict houses, felt that her family's homes "grew out of the earth."

Benedict and his wife divorced in 1930. He moved to a home built by his in-laws on Grant Street in Denver, though he kept his ties to Littleton. Following his divorce, Benedict traveled to China and other exotic regions in the Far East, which seemed to enhance his social appeal. Both Benedict and his wife, June were collectors of art, and both gave fine collections of paintings to museums.

Benedict was successful throughout his life, and later made his home at the Colburn Hotel in downtown Denver. He died in 1948 at the age of sixty-nine and is buried in the Littleton Cemetery.

Odd Interlacings

It doesn't take long in researching these castles, to determine that the great majority in Colorado were built in the space of some two decades, and often within two or three years of each other. Denver was fetal, even embryonic during this early period, and wide open to the driving ego, particularly if that ego were attached to a bright and imaginative brain. These egos were most frequently male, and it wasn't uncommon for your best friend to foreclose on your property or walk off with your wife, or maybe both. (Diametrically opposite these super egos is John Sutton who is responsible for the South Broadway Christian Church, giving quite literally his all, to create a memorial for his wife and a gift for his community. And the architect? Ta-da! William Lang.)

Speaking of egos, please note the percentage of divorce in this (former) bunch, and the re-coupling of the male with a female who was likewise. This inevitably resulted in a resounding ostracism by the Denver self-appointed Alphas, or the "Sacred Thirty-Six," but then, who can name

that group today, when those who gained social Pariah-ship are still written about and extolled. Who says that crime doesn't pay?

Because these men were a special breed, they did indeed, flock together. Eliza Hughes, daughter of William Hughes of Kittredge Castle, married John Springer of Springer Castle, and her daughter Annie inherited both castles upon the deaths of her father and grandfather. Springer's second wife, Isabelle, was a doozy, as well as a floozy, and collided with Henry C. Brown by having one lover murder another in his very reputable bar, in the very high class Brown Palace.

Charles Kittredge, having lost his castle in the 1893 depression, moved into a home at 755 Oneida Street, built by our beloved architect, William Lang. In fact, it would probably be the majority of these castle-builders who were undone by the great silver collapse—Richthofen, Kittredge, Lang, John Walker, and Brown, down but not out. And on the up side, it was the silver collapse that most certainly stimulated the town of Leadville to create their Crystal Castle.

Col. William Palmer, our Glen Eyrie fellow, collided with several here. A railroad builder, he was also seeking to develop the area dominated by John Cleveland Osgood of Redstone fame, but Osgood prevailed. Interestingly, Palmer, who created the Denver and Rio Grande Railroad, needed access across Indian land in Santa Fe, when Father Francolon was the priest there. It was Francolon, builder of Miramont Castle, who gained that access for him.

Of course, the ubiquitous architect, Jock Benedict, had his finger in every pie. He was involved with the Summer White House, the renovation of the Springer Castle under Kistler, and in 1924, William Grant hired him to add a wing to the Richthofen Castle.

Speaking of William Grant, it was he, the physician, who looked after von Phul, the lover, who was murdered in the Brown Palace bar.

Interestingly, several originally came from Ohio, as did Henry Brown, Charles Kittredge, and William Lang. Both Henry Brown and John Cleveland Osgood were orphaned at a tender age.

Divorces were everywhere. In fact, it's easier to list those who *didn't* divorce their first mates: General William Palmer was exceptionally gallant and upright, of course. Father Francolon never married, and Jim Bishop has been with his Pheobe since 1962. Several also lost wives to early death: Springer's wife, Annie, General Palmer's "Queen," and Kittredge's Sadie—not a one reached the age of forty.

The subject of curses is interesting. Miramont is the most spine-tingling, with the nun who chastised Father Francolon dying a hideous death. Another priestly curse came down on John Brisben Walker, who dared to rename the Garden of Angels, the Garden of the Titans. He ended up with *three* burned castles: River Front burned from internal combustion, and his Falcon Castle was struck by lightning, as was the Summer White House, though it hardly got off the ground.

Several of our castles here are contemporary. These seem to have been built not as a show of power but simply because the builders liked castles. But these too were built by men of incredible ambition, who often created their structures through their own efforts.

Throughout castledom, dragons and lions seem to proliferate, with Bishop's breathing fire, as the displaced one at Dunafon did. Redstone has two smaller dragons, but lots of lions. Winner in the lion department is The Lion and the Rose, which has statues, pictures and fountains dedicated to the King of Beasts.

So it seems that castle makers do have a lot in common, whatever their era. In the twenty-first century, who would ever believe there were so many castles in Colorado?

Below are the castles that do offer services and accommodations to the public. Please note that most of these facilities require prior notice, particularly for the formal afternoon teas.

Location	Teas	Tours	Events	Accommodations
Cherokee Ranch 6113 No. Daniels Pk Sedalia, CO 80135 303-688-5555	Wed. 2 P.M. $40	W,Th,S 9:30 A.M.	Yes	No
Dunafon Castle Idledale, CO 303-378-1533	No	Arranged	Yes	No
Glen Eyrie 3820 No. 30th Col. Sprgs, CO 80904 1-800-944-4536	Yes 2:30P.M. $20	Yes 1:00P.M. $3–$5	Yes All year Open	Yes All Year $70–$170
Castle Marne 1572 Race St. Denver, CO 80206 1-800-92MARNE	Yes	No	No	Yes – B&B
Miramont Castle 9 Capitol Hill Ave. Manitou Spgs, 80829 719-685-1011	3 PM $17 T,F,S	Yes 10–4 P.M.	No	Food Available Open 11–4 T-S
Redstone Castle 58 Redstone Blvd. Redstone, CO 81623 970-963-9656	No	F–M 1:30 P.M. $15, $10	No	Pending
Springer Castle 9900 So. Ranch Rd. Highlands Ranch, CO 80126 303-791-2500	No	No	Yes	No

See the following pages for the specifics on EVENTS and ACCOMMODATIONS.

Cherokee Ranch and Castle is available for corporate events, weddings, or special occasions by contacting 303-688-5555.

In addition to the weekly high teas, special seasonal teas are also available. Brunches and lunches can be arranged for groups of from twenty to fifty people.

The castle also sponsors a Performing Arts Series running from May through December. These gala events are comprised of three parts: Part 1 is a complimentary wine tasting and cash bar with a buffet supper and informal tours of the castle; Part 2 is the performance of an outstanding artist or group; and Part 3 is a dessert/coffee reception allowing conversation with the performers. Performances are held either on the castle veranda or inside the castle and are priced accordingly. For information on ticket prices, either series packages or individual purchases, call 303-688-4600 or visit their website at www.cherokeeranch.org.

As a foundation and hand-in-hand with Douglas County Open Space, Cherokee Ranch and Castle's mission is to devote itself to western heritage, wildlife, and the arts. Besides sponsoring castle tours for school children, many opportunities are available to study wildlife and conservation. For a schedule, call 303-688-5555.

Dunafon Castle is available for weddings, corporate special events, or fund raisers, but it is advised to schedule well ahead of time. Dates for an event can be scheduled and held for a ten-day period before parties are obligated to a contract. After this period of time a contract is agreed upon or the date will be released.

If a group of fifteen or more persons wish to schedule a tour only of the castle, this can be arranged at a cost of $20 per person.

For further information or to make a reservation, contact Annette Gilman, Charity Event Manager, at 303-378-1533, or go online at guest@dunafon castle.com.

Glen Eyrie is the world headquarters and conference ministry for The Navigators, an international, non-denominational Christian organization. Although focused on Christian "Life Changing" Retreats, the castle and grounds are open and available to the public and offer overnight or weekly accommodations. Public and private teas and tours are held daily, but reservations are necessary. To make a reservation, call 1-800-944-GLEN (4536).

Glen Eyrie is the focus of many Christian programs to inspire, build, and encourage leadership, parenting, and marital bonds. The 880+ acre campus and 67-room castle can be reserved for just about any size group, up to 250. Contact them at 1-800-944-GLEN (4536) or 719-634-0808.

Weddings are also very popular and many extras are available, such as horse-drawn carriage rides and gourmet catering. For information, contact The Castle Wedding Planner at 1-800-944-GLEN (4536).

For fifty years, The Navigators have provided a summer camp for children eight to eighteen on Eagle Lake. Kids are divided into two groups, eight to fourteen and fourteen to Eighteen, and the camp runs Sunday afternoon until the following Friday morning. The program offers hiking, horse back riding, camping, and excursions, as well as Bible study. Call 1-800-US-EAGLE or visit their website; www.eaglelake.org.

Two of the most popular yearly Christmas events are the Madrigal Banquet and Colorado Springs Chamber Orchestra "Christmas Throughout the Ages," held on several dates from November until Christmas. The elegant Banquet is a renaissance celebration, complete with costumes, a five-course meal of appropriate foods, and entertainment, celebrated in the castle's Great Hall, complete with gigantic Christmas tree and all the trimmings. Tickets for all holiday shows go on sale starting in August, and because of high demand, are often sold out by mid November. Call 1-877-488-8787 or contact www.GlenEyrie.org.

Springer Castle is owned and run by the Shea Company, the developers who bought the entire Highlands Ranch area in 1997. They allot the Highlands Ranch Community Association ten events per year, which include a father-daughter ball, a mother-son ball, a volunteer dinner, Mother's Day, Highlands Ranch Days—a three-day event, and a jazz concert. The Metro District of Highlands Ranch holds an annual Christmas Party on the first Saturday in December. For information call Jamie Noebel at 303-791-2500.

Also holding events is the Highlands Ranch Historical Society. For information on the society and their programs contact Caroline Smith at 303-471-5611.

ACCOMMODATIONS

Glen Eyrie offers economy lodgings in auxiliary buildings or premium rooms in the castle itself. Lodgings include a large breakfast buffet in the castle to all patrons every morning from 8:00 A.M. until 10:00 A.M. Prices may vary depending on the season and availability. Call 1-800-944-4536.

Castle Marne is a carefully replicated Victorian home turned bed and breakfast near downtown Denver, and close to all Denver attractions. Greet the morning with homemade breads and muffins, special-blend coffee and a complete gourmet breakfast. A game room with pool table, darts, and board games, and a library are available if you wish to hang around for the day. Or stroll the Victorian garden, maybe playing a game of croquet. Evening service provides a complimentary tea, coffee, or soft drink on the veranda. Prices vary from $105 to $260 for accommodations. Call 303-331-0621 or 1-800-92MARNE. Website www.castlemarne.com.

Miramont Castle has a delightful tearoom called the Queen's Parlour, open Tuesday through Saturday from 11:00 A.M. until 4:00 P.M. serving "hearty Victorian lunches" of homemade soups, cobblers, desserts, and sandwiches. High tea is served in winter on Tuesday through Saturday at 12:00 P.M. and 3:00 P.M. and in summer on Tuesday, Friday and Saturday only. It consists of a variety of hot teas, scones with lemon curd, Devonshire cream, and an assortment of veggies, fruit, sandwiches, and desserts. *For high tea, reservations are required with two days notice.* The cost is $20. Call 719-685-1011.

Redstone Castle, as of this printing, is open only for tours. Tickets can be bought at three locations in Redstone: the General Store, Tiffany's of Redstone, and The Crystal Club, all on the main road.

It is planned for the castle to become a luxury resort with overnight accommodations. The resort will include a full-service spa, pool, conservatory, fine dining, and upscale bar, to be open to the public as well as the hotel guests. Weddings and special events are in the offing, and for updates, call 970-963-9656 or visit their website at redstone castle@yahoo.com.

GLOSSARY

Bailey — a large, flat yard inside the castle guard wall.

Barbican — a defensive work in front of a castle entrance.

Buttress — the supports at the base of the castle walls.

Cantilevered — an overhang of an upper story; a projection beyond what is below.

Castellated — furnished with turrets and battlements in the style of a castle.

Chamfered — beveled, as cutting off the edge or corner.

Concentric — a castle-type with an outside wall beyond an inner wall.

Crenelated — the top of the castle wall punctuated with even gaps; such as a trowel for mortar.

Donjon — a square keep. This word later became the underground prison, or dungeon.

Frieze — a large, horizontal stripe of decoration painted next to the ceiling.

Gothic — from the Goths, a Germanic style of the Middle Ages; a design of window or doorway culminating in a pointed arch.

Great Hall — the large inner room in the keep where the living took place.

Groined Vault — the curved edge of the junction of two intersecting vaults. Triangular sections of ceiling curved to meet at their tips, as does the human groin.

Keep — the main tower containing a watchtower and family living quarters.

Machicolations — gaps in a cantilevered overhang, used to drop hot oil on the enemy.

Motte — a hill on which the main structure was erected.

Oriel — a projecting bay window, supported from below.

Palisade — a wooden fence.

Porte-cochere — an archway built to allow a carriage to pass through; an entrance to a grand home.

Portico — a large porch, often with columns.

Rhyolite — a glassy, volcanic rock, similar to granite and native to Colorado.

Richardson — named after architect H. H. Richardson, the style was developed in the late 1880s and reflected the size and splendor of the western landscape using massive stone walls and rounded arches on otherwise Victorian structures. It was characterized by excessive and elaborate ornamentation and usually combined with Romanesque.

Romanesque — a style of architecture popular in the eleventh to twelfth centuries and was based on the architecture used by the ancient Romans with thick, massive walls and interior bays.

Tabernacle — a large tent, usually used as a temporary church.

Terrazzo — a mosaic flooring consisting of small pieces of marble or granite set in mortar and given a high polish.

Turret—a small, ornamented tower or projection on a building, often on a castle.

Tor — a rocky pinnacle of a hill or mountain.

PHOTO CREDITS

Unless otherwise indicated, the photos were taken by the author.

COVER PHOTO: Photo of Dunafon Castle, courtesy of Mike Dunafon.

INTRODUCTION: Art work on pp. xii, xiv, and xv by Rebecca Finkel. The Dreamstime Agency supplied the following photos: Tower of London, p. xiv, © James Talbot, photographer, and Neuschwanstein, p. xv, © FreesurF69, photographer.

DUNAFON CASTLE photos taken by and courtesy of Mike Dunafon and Steven Crisilius, except photos on pp. 12 (lower), 19, and 22.

RICHTHOFEN CASTLE: Pp. 36–37, 42, 45, courtesy of Jerry Priddy. Barbarossa, (38), interior, (39), music room (40), and dining room (44), Denver Public Library, Western History Collection. Page 43 photos by Decker Westerberg.

SPRINGER CASTLE: Photos on pp. 54–64 taken by and courtesy of Jamie Noebel.

GLEN EYRIE: Photos on pp. 66–67, 68 (lower) 71–73, 75 (top), courtesy of the Glen Eyrie Group, a Ministry of the Navigators.

MIRAMONT CASTLE: Photo of original castle (82) courtesy of the Manitou Springs Historical Society.

CASTLE EYRIE: Old castle (105), archives of the Denver Public Library, Western History Collection.

THE CASTLE AT RIVER FRONT: Photos on pp. 140–142, 144, the Denver Public Library, Western History Collection.

CRYSTAL CASTLE: Photos on pp. 146–149, 152, the Denver Public Library, Western History Collection. Photo on p. 151 by the author, courtesy of the National Mining Museum in Leadville, Colorado.

CUTTHROAT CASTLE: Photos on pp. 154–155 courtesy of Chris Nickel, Lead Ranger at Hovenweep National Monument, National Park Service.

FALCON CASTLE: Photos on pp. 162 and 163, the Denver Public Library, Western History Collection.

KITTREDGE CASTLE: Photos on pp. 168–71, 173, the Denver Public Library, Western History Collection.

SUMMER WHITE HOUSE: Photos on pp. 174, 176–79, the Denver Public Library, Western History Collection.

BIBLIOGRAPHY

Books

Appleby, Susan Consola, *Fading Past, The Story of Douglas County, Colorado*, Filter Press, LLC, Palmer Lake, CO.

Blair, Edward, *Palace of Ice*, Timberline Books, Leadville, CO, 1972.

Brettell, Richard R., *Historic Denver, 1858–1893*, Publication of Historic Denver.

Bretz, James, *Mansions of Denver 1870–1938*, Pruett Publishing Co., Boulder, CO, 1948.

Clark, Richard, *Castles*, The Bookwright Press, N.Y., 1986.

Copp, Shirley, *Miramont Castle*, Manitou Springs Historical Society, 1985.

Coquoz, Rene L., *King Pleasure Ruled in 1896*, Johnson Books, Boulder, CO, 1969.

Eastwood, Kay, *Life in a Castle*, Crabtree Publishing Co., N.Y., Ontario, Oxford, UK, 2003.

Everett, Derek R., *The Colorado State Capitol*, University Press of Colorado, Boulder, CO, 2005.

Fagan, Brian, *Chaco Canyon*, Oxford University Press, N.Y., 2005.

Hunt, Corinne, *The Brown Palace—Denver's Grande Dame*, Denver Historical Society, 2003.

Kohl, Edith Eudora, *Denver's Historic Mansions*, Sage Books, Denver, CO, 1957.

Kreck, Dick, *Murder at the Brown Palace*, Fulcrum Publishing Co., Golden, CO, 2003.

Macaulay, David, *CASTLE*, Houghton Mifflin Co., Boston, MA, 1977.

MacDonald, Fiona, James, John, and Antram, David, *A Samurai Castle*, Peter Bedrick Books, N.Y., 1998.

Marr, Josephine L., *Douglas County—A Historical Journey*, B&B Printers, Gunnison, CO, 1983.

Noel, Thomas J., *Richthofen's Montclair*, Pruett Publishing Co., Boulder, CO, 1978.

Sacred Stones: Colorado's Red Rocks Park and Ampitheatre, Colorado Book Review Center, March 2005.

Noel, Thomas J., and Hansen, William J., *The Park Hill Neighborhood*, Historic Denver, Denver, CO, 2002.

Ruland, Sylvia, *The Lion of Redstone*, Johnson Books, Boulder, CO, 1981.

Seiden, O.J., *Denver's Richthofen Castle*, Stonehenge Books, Boulder, CO, 1980.

Sheehan, Sean, *Castles*, Smart Apple Media, No. Mankato, MN, 2005.

Sims, Lesley, *The Usborne Book of Castles*, Usborne Internet, 2003.

Unstead, R. J., *A Castle*, Warwick Press, Griswold & Dempsey LTD, Hong Kong, 1986.

Weir, Darlene Godat, *Leadville's Ice Palace*, Gilliland Press, Arkansas City, KS, 1994.

Foundation and Society's Publications

Denver Foundation for Architecture, *Guide to Denver Architecture*, Westcliff Publishers, Englewood, CO, 2001.

Historic Society of Idaho Springs, *Trailings, Tracks and Tommyknockers, The History of Clear Creek County*, 1986.

Magazine and Newspaper Articles

American Heritage Magazine, "The Summer White House in the Clouds," Francis Russell, October, 1973.

Colorado Heritage, "J. J. B. Benedict and His Magnificent Unbuilt Buildings," Dan W. Corson. Summer, 1997.

Denver Monthly Magazine, "The Richthofen Castle," Janis Kincaid, Vol. 9, #1, May, 1980.

The Denver Post
"W. W. Grant Sells Castle," April 8, 1934.
"Saving Mansions a 'Neighborly' Gesture," Joanne Ditmer, August 24, 1977.
"Uptown on Hill tour to include castles that are just like home," Joanne Ditmer, Sept. 8, 1989.
"Castle for sale—in Denver," Steve Raabe, Aug. 28, 1998.
The Denver Republican, " John Miller Passes Away," June 20, 1902.

Evergreen Magazine, "John Brisben Walker, the Man and the Myth, Parts I and II," Catherine Dittman, Fall-Winter, 1978, Spring-Summer, 1979.

Homes and Life Styles Magazine, "A Trek Through Historical Colorado Architecture," Cathleen Norman, Apr. 1994.

Mountain Commuter, "The Man's Dream was the Castle," Kathleen E. Murphy, October, 1982.

Rocky Mountain News
Rocky Mountain Memories, "Time shatters tycoon's dream of a Colorado White House," Frances Melrose, July 10, 1983.
"Large Purchase Near Morrison," October 18, 1906.
"Richthofen Castle sacked by vandals," Nov. 2, 1982.
"The Baron's Bower," Frances Melrose, Aug. 15, 1993.
"Awards for Efficient Energy Use to be Presented," May 10, 1980.
"Castle on the Platte," Herndon Davis, May 21, 1950.

Internet

"John Brisben Walker, the Man and Mt. Morrison," historicredrocks.org

Findagrave.com

HistoricDenverCollection.org

HauntedInnsFor Sale.html

Photoswest.org/exhib/lang/index.html.

Richthofen Castle: www.dupontcastles.com.

Castlemarne.com

Mollybrown.org

Neighborhood Link/Montclair, www.myonline neighborhood.com

Interviews

Meg Anderson (Cherokee Castle)
Lisa Barnes (Dunafon Castle)
Jim Bishop (Bishop Castle)
B. J. Ellison (Walker Castle)
Mike Dunafon (Dunafon Castle)
Dominic (Cano) Espinosa (Cano's Castle)
Darlene Godat (Leadville's Crystal Castle)
Meme and Doc Hardin (Hardin Castle)
John Hill (Cherokee Castle)
Susan McEvoy (Redstone Castle)
Sally Cooper Murray (Richthofen Castle)
Chris Nickel (Hovenweep)
Jamie Noebel (Springer Castle)
Jim and Diane Peiker (Castle Marne)
Jerry Priddy (Richthofen Castle)
Caroline Smith (Springer Castle)
Chris Vitt (South Broadway Christian Church)